From Surviving *to* Thriving

FABIANA BACCHINI

A mother's journey through
infertility, loss and miracles

To my sons

Thomas, Michael and Gabriel

PRAISE REVIEWS

"Whether you are experiencing life challenges yourself, work with those who are, or are just curious about the amazing capacity of the human spirit, this book will open your eyes and give you a new perspective. As you read it, you can't help but feel your heart grow bigger with love and gratitude."

Dr. Linda S. Franck, Professor of Pediatric Nursing,
University of California, San Francisco

"Fabiana's wonderful book intertwines the birth of her preemie son with her candid experiences of exploring the world to find herself, and her love and marriage. I could not put her book down. It affected me profoundly.

I have had the privilege of meeting and spending some time with her. I am amazed that she can volunteer daily to support parents of preemies, while looking after her special needs child. Most people cannot believe that parents who have experienced difficulties and stresses paradoxically become stronger, feel better about themselves, and give more to society. Fabiana is a stellar example of such an exceptional parent."

Saroj Saigal MD, author of the book, "Preemie voices", Friesen

"I am moved by her journey and the courage she has to walk her own path.... It is a wonderful way of encouraging people to find and walk and learn from their own."

Joan Emery, teacher and writer

"*From Surviving to Thriving* is a powerful read that will take you through the diversity of life experiences that lead to a rich, full life. Fabiana's writing articulates how beauty and joy can be found even in the midst of the most challenging and heartbreaking situations. She takes readers through her thought process and what made her grow. She encourages readers to re-examine their lives by looking inwards and shifting their perspective. Their empowering story demonstrates how loss and sadness can inspire us to be the best versions of ourselves and is a must-read for anyone who is hoping to do the same."

Anchel Krishna, freelance writer and consultant

"Fabiana's story of her life journey with a premature baby is truly touching, personal and so full of courage, hope and love as only a mother can express! A truly remarkable story with lessons for all of us."

Dr. Shoo Lee, Paediatrician-in-Chief for the Sinai Health System and Director of the Maternal-Infant Research Centre at Mount Sinai Hospital.

"I have witnessed Fabiana's transformation into the courageous, resilient and powerful woman that she is today. What strikes me the most about her is how she handles everything with immense grace. We can learn a lot of what it truly means to be a woman, a wife and a mother by reading her story. She reminds us that our power lies within us and that all we have to do is look for it, especially when we struggle."

Gina Mollicone-Long, Best-selling Author and Creator of Greatness U

FOREWORD

I don't think Fabiana expected to become such a huge influence on others when she started out on her journey. When I first met her and her husband, Stel, they were learning to adjust to having their baby, Gabriel, at home with them after spending nearly 5 months in the NICU. What I have since witnessed, has been nothing short of inspirational.

I've had the privilege of being Fabi's business coach and mentor, but first and foremost, her friend; and I have to confess, I think I got the better end of the deal. She has taught me so much about moving through the trials of life with dignity and grace, and finding joy and laughter when things don't go as planned.

Her journey didn't begin with Gabriel's birth though; his birth was more of an exclamation point on a journey filled with lessons and courage. Instead, it began when she proved to be a ferocious and unrelenting advocate. Whenever she heard the words 'It's not possible', Fabi looked for another avenue or tried a different approach. To say that she was unstoppable would be an understatement.

The journey was not all roses either. The experiences were tough - at times heart-breaking - and the road filled with insurmountable obstacles, but she and her family found their way to a new equilibrium, always returning to gratitude for the extraordinary life handed to them.

The choices Fabi made were based on finding ways to grow and give back. Whether it was empowering young women, building a full access playground for Gabriel's school, or starting a charity to help other families facing long stays in the NICU, she has always been one of the most generous individuals I know.

Through each step of her incredible journey, she has applied the valuable lessons that she writes about in her book and allowed us to share her exceptional story on an intimate level. Although she may not have set out with the goal of becoming a role model to others facing adversity, Fabi has managed to touch everyone she meets with her effortless grace and class.

Teresa Easler
Founder of Connect to The Core

Bio

Fabiana is an accomplished journalist and speaker. Originally from Brazil, she moved to Toronto in pursuit of a higher purpose and after facing her own challenges with infertility, began to advocate for families with adversities. She currently volunteers in the NICU at Mount Sinai Hospital where she continues to help educate and support other families. She is the founder of Handfull Hearts.

www.handfullhearts.com
www.fabianabacchini.com

CHAPTER 1
Surviving

"A difficult time can be more readily endured if we retain the conviction that our existence holds a purpose - a cause to pursue, a person to love, a goal to achieve."

— *John Maxwell*

MAY 16, 2012

With a swollen body, I struggled out of bed. At three o'clock in the morning, sleep was eluding me, a pervasive cough was worsening and my breathing became laboured. In an effort to allow my husband to sleep, I made my way downstairs to our family room. I was also hoping that more open space would allow me to breathe freely and eventually return to sleep. I was uncomfortable; my body was heavy with 40 pounds of extra weight, my legs were twice their normal circumference and my back was aching.

A year previous, we had moved into our beautiful home. I still marveled every morning when I was awake early enough to see the sunrise through the big windows creating rainbows on the floor. That day was no different, except for the fact that I wasn't well.

Throughout the early morning hours, I continued to cough. At around six o'clock, I started coughing continuously and intensely for about twenty minutes. When the coughing ceased, I felt a strange and warm wetness beneath me. I stood up and looked at the couch in disbelief. Walking toward the stairs, I was calling my husband, Stel, leaving a trail of blood as I walked. Waves of fear enveloped me. Stel came to me quickly, hearing the emotion in my voice. I noticed his face. He was attempting to appear composed, but I knew my husband well. I could see the terror under the facade of calm. We needed to get to the hospital quickly. Stel helped me to shower, washing away the blood, then helped me dress. Time seemed to stop, slow down and speed up all at once.

My mom was visiting from Brazil, so she packed a bag with a few necessities for me and would be able to stay with our three-year-old son, Thomas, while we were at the hospital. She too looked frightened. I asked her to clean the floor before Thomas woke up and we headed out the door, destined for the emergency department at Mount Sinai Hospital. Intuitively, I knew I was not coming home for a while. Maybe, deeper inside, I had a knowingness that things were about to change in a more profound way.

In silence, my husband and I made the thirty-minute drive from the West End of the city to downtown Toronto. We had been making the same trip at least twice weekly for the last six weeks; this time it seemed longer. Life seemed to proceed for everyone that we passed, but it seemed that mine had stopped. Complete silence. In my mind, a black and white movie was playing at a very fast speed. Looking through the car window, I saw what was happening outside. There were people rushing to work, others waiting for the bus, and women pushing baby strollers. Simultaneously, other images started to pop in my head. All the events that happened during my first pregnancy started to come alive. I had enjoyed every second of my highly anticipated first pregnancy. I watched every centimeter of my belly grow, taking photos each week to see the change. I read a book detailing what the baby developed each week: the organs, the skin, the nails, the hair. Every day was a blessing, every morning sickness was celebrated because we had waited so long. Life felt so complete at that time. Stel and I anxiously waited to meet and look into the eyes of our first child. I was overwhelmed to watch my body transform, feeling the kicks and seeing the waves the baby created beneath my skin.

Stel was in love with my belly. He constantly spoke to the baby. When we found out it was a baby boy, he started planning to take him to soccer games, hockey games, the lessons he would enroll him in and everything he could teach him.

I was working part time and spent a lot of time shopping for furniture and decorations for the nursery. I researched the latest baby items. I bought cute baby boy outfits, tiny shoes and so many other items I found essential, of course most of them weren't. I was in awe that a life was growing inside me. It felt like a miracle, how a human being could create another one.

Everyone around me was excited as it was a long ride to conceive. My friends organized a baby shower for me. We received so many gifts, but it wasn't about the gifts, it was about celebrating life and the things we can accomplish when we believe we can, despite the difficulties.

During the pregnancy, I dreamed about a life of possibilities for my little son and I was looking forward to hear him calling me Mama. Past my due date, I was counting down the hours to start feeling my first contractions, to finally meet my baby. He was 10 days late. When I started feeling the contractions early one morning, I had a rush of excitement running through my body. My parents were visiting, anxiously awaiting the birth of their first grandson. After a long but happy labour, holding the hand of my husband, I heard a loud cry. I cried too. It was real, it was very real. My excitement was indescribable. The nurse brought him to me wrapped in a blue blanket and placed him in my arms, introducing my baby boy to me and calling me Mommy. I immediately felt immense unconditional love for my son. A love I didn't know was possible. We were now a family.

My mind kept flipping from the current moment to these images of my first pregnancy, which seemed like a distant dream. Tears were falling down my cheeks. I feared what was to come; I feared the unknown. More silence, more lives passing as we drove.

Upon arriving at the emergency department of Mount Sinai Hospital, I was immediately sent to maternity triage on the seventh floor. From there I was sent to the high-risk pregnancy ward, known as 7-south, where I was given a small, private room. We had made these arrangements previously in case anything unforeseen occurred, and now here we were on 7-south in a high-risk situation. A few nurses came into our room to assess me and to obtain my history. My obstetrician was surprised to see me there so soon after our last scheduled appointment. He ordered a Doppler ultrasound on my legs to determine the cause and extent of the swelling, and I stayed at the hospital overnight.

MAY 17, 2012

I was given medication in the morning; by the afternoon I was experiencing severe pain and cramping. I became angry because I believed that the pain was due to the medication. The nurse examined me and to my surprise I was in active labour, four centimeters dilated. I had been in labour before with my first child. I knew the pain, but I guess at that moment I couldn't perceive that I was in labour as I was only 26 weeks pregnant, 14 weeks ahead of my due date. The doctor that was on-call told me that there wasn't anything that could be done to stop the labour. Again, my perception of time was altered.

Various doctors began to discuss possible delivery options with Stel and myself. I was in excruciating pain. They came to us to explain all the different procedures and options: normal delivery, Caesarean section (commonly referred to as C-section), and anesthesia. Whichever decision we made had to be fast. Things were progressing very rapidly and they wanted to make sure the delivery was safe for the baby and for me. The on-call doctor explained that if I opted for a C-section they would do a vertical incision. At that moment in time, my thoughts travelled to not being able to wear a two-piece swimsuit ever again. I wouldn't want to show such a personal and tragic scar so publicly. Then I laughed at myself, as in that critical situation I was concerned about hiding my story. That scar would be a permanent reminder of that day, regardless of its orientation on my body.

The safest option was a C-section, so I was rushed to the operating room. Screaming and contorting with pain, I forced myself to sit still for the spinal anesthesia. To ground myself, I asked if I could hold the nurse to help keep me still. I had to calm my mind, regulate my breathing and imagine my feet rooted on the ground, even though I was sitting on a bed in the operating room. She allowed me to wrap my arms around her as I was grounding my mind. I focused on and visualized a successful delivery. Immediately the labour pain ceased.

I was ready for the procedure that would forever change our lives. A very caring nurse whispered all the events that were about to happen in my ears. "You are going to feel a push, and now… here comes Twin A." Michael, Twin A, had passed away the week before. From my left side, I watched the nurse cleaning him and wrapping him in a blanket. She then placed him in my arms. My baby, my Michael, was stillborn. Stel's eyes met mine. Together we cried silently for our second child who was no longer with us. At that moment, the song *Let Me Fall* recorded by Cirque du Soleil played in my head, specifically the part when it says, "There's a moment when fear and dreams must collide." That was the moment for me.

I do not recall Gabriel being born, but I noticed everyone apprehensive for his delivery. I have a vague memory of the doctor holding him for forty-five seconds before cutting the umbilical cord.

The rush now was to save Twin B, Gabriel, who was immediately taken to the resuscitation room before I could lay my eyes on him. There were no cries from my newborn babies, no happy tears, no celebration, no doctors or nurses congratulating me on the birth of my children. Just more silence.

I was transferred to the recovery area with my husband and my baby, Michael, who was very tiny and seemed to be sleeping peacefully. Nothing made sense to me.

I don't remember seeing Gabriel when the nurses brought him to me in an incubator. I saw pictures, months later, of him inside the incubator. His body was wrapped in a plastic bag to regulate his temperature. Subsequently, he was rushed into the Neonatal Intensive Care Unit.

The NICU at Mount Sinai Hospital was to be our home for the next 146 days.

CHAPTER 2
Leading to Today

"The beginning is the most important part of the work."

− Plato

Born and raised in São Paulo, Brazil, to a middle-class family, I had a typical childhood. Across from our condo was a magnificent park and green space where all the neighbourhood children loved to congregate and create magical worlds to play in. Parks in Brazil are almost magical, so lush and green. The sounds of birds singing from the sky-scraping trees, the constant sound of the insects humming in the underbrush and the beautiful breezes breaking up the heat. There couldn't have been a better place to start my life.

My parents instilled life lessons, morals and values in my younger brother and myself from a very young age, using our surrounding environment as the textbook. The first lesson they taught us was the value of education; they sacrificed financially to send my brother and me to a private school. While all of my neighbours attended public schools, my parents saw that the private schools provided a richer learning environment. It was on the school bus in kindergarten where I learned my first lesson.

The older girls on the school bus made fun of me because I was from a middle-class neighbourhood, while all the other kids were from the wealthy suburbs of São Paulo. I cried every time they taunted me and threw my lunch out of a window of the bus. My mother turned this into a learning situation by teaching me to speak up for myself and to not care what other people thought of me.

While the girls on the bus were nasty, the kids in my class were different. They were nice to me; they were my friends. When we had play dates, they loved coming over and playing in the wonderful park across the street from my place.

Driving through the beautiful and wealthy neighbourhoods, seeing beautifully designed homes and brand new cars made me dream of being financially successful when I grew up. I recall experiencing the feeling of wealth by going to friends' weekend homes by the beach and having their housekeepers prepare snacks for us. I knew I wanted more.

My father was an economic advisor, working long hours in the financial department of a retail company. Eventually, after I had grown up, he made his way to be vice-president of a prestigious lingerie company. My parents had a true partnership. While my dad worked, my mom ensured that my brother and I had the best care and a comfortable home. We were always a very close family, spending a lot of time together. On long weekends, we would travel to the countryside to enjoy nature and time with friends. Other weekends we would venture to the beach, going on long walks, long bike rides and tasting different foods.

Looking back, I realized that my passion for travelling and food started right there as a child. The first time I travelled by plane was with my grandmother to the Northeast of Brazil to spend one month with my aunt who was living there at the time. I still remember being on the plane and the days I spent with my aunt - who is now ninety years old - and my cousins. I had the time of my life picking mangoes from the large trees and sightseeing in the historic city of Salvador.

My mom's dream was to travel the world, but she couldn't afford it. Many of our conversations were about travelling abroad. One of my mom's first cousins had married a man from the United States, and every time she returned from travelling there, we would go to her house. She told us the stories of her trip, what life was like in her husband's small Kentucky town. I was amazed and curious, wanting to discover the world's treasures as well.

As we couldn't afford expensive trips, my parents gave us the opportunity to travel around São Paulo where there are incredible places to explore. Every winter, the temperature may drop down to ten degrees Celsius at night for a few days. Each winter we went to a town in the mountains three hours away from São Paulo. The town is known as the Switzerland of Brazil. The architecture was inspired by the Swiss chalets. It was very clean and the gardens were very European. It was colder in the evenings and everybody enjoyed adding jackets to their outfits. After living in Canada, I laugh as that cold weather is like a mild spring day in Toronto. We had a great time there as a family, hiking, horseback riding and going to the top of the mountain on a lift. It was a special place for my parents as it was their honeymoon spot.

We also spent a lot of time at the beach in the summer and almost every long weekend. One of my aunts had a house on the seaside; we loved going there. It was in a historic town (there are many in Brazil), from the time when the Portuguese had colonized my home country. My gastronomic adventures were further fostered there as I tried a lot of seafood that wasn't widely available in São Paulo.

By my teen years, my parents' economic situation was better, allowing them to purchase a cottage. We loved going there every weekend, having barbeques and swimming in the nearby river. I also loved having friends over from the surrounding cottages each evening.

Near the end of high school, I started to dream about going to England to learn English. I thank my mom for creating a curiosity in me about the world, and for sparking the desire to travel. By example, my parents strove to show us that for a successful life, it was essential to work hard to accomplish our goals. They showed us that studying would open doors to success. My dad always said that whatever I decided to be, to keep my values and be the best at what I chose.

My parents ingrained a strong appreciation for life and gratitude for the things we had. There were always people, on our very doorstep, struggling to live. I saw my parents' lifelong commitment to make the lives of others better. My mother helped everyone around her. Several times, my mother allowed a homeless woman from our neighbourhood to sleep in our garage on cold nights. She would bring homeless kids into our condo and allow them to shower, then feed them and give them our old clothing. I think my mom would keep them all if we had a large enough house. I remember her saying that if we had more money we could give more, help more. She saw no difference between people; she embraced everyone and cared for everyone equally. I started to see the world this way as well and dreamed about making the world a better place. I couldn't understand how some had so much and others so little. This may be the greatest lesson a parent can teach their children.

My mother ensured that my brother and I were involved with several community initiatives from a very early age. Christmas was particularly fun for all of us. My cousin would dress up as Santa and we would go to poor areas distributing toys and food that we had collected for the months leading up to Christmas. This was the highlight of our holidays. We didn't care about what we received as gifts; we just wanted to see the happy faces of the families receiving our gifts. Those were the days that I saw my mom feeling very fulfilled, so happy.

Later, I discovered why Christmas was so important for my mom. She was raised in a poor family. With three kids, my grandparents struggled to make ends meet. My mom told me that when she started to work in a factory at the age of 13, she bought a doll with her first paycheque. She had never received a toy for Christmas so she bought her own. It all made sense to me when I saw her coming alive during the Christmas holidays, giving away toys to children who were having the same childhood she had.

Being exposed to social differences made me want to make a difference in people's lives. It made me want to change the world. I watched movies of people doing great things to better humanity. I wanted to be like them. I wondered where one person could start to accomplish such a large goal. I started writing all my goals in my diary. Many of the things that I wrote, back then, seemed impossible. I wanted to travel the world. I wanted to have a successful career. I wanted to make the world a better place.

Journalism was the key. By high school I believed the only possibility of attaining all my goals was by becoming a journalist. It would be my way to contribute, to give the people a voice, to illustrate the injustices that I saw every morning and evening on my own doorstep. I was hoping that as the world read and saw, someone would act and the process of change would commence. I was a dreamer. Perhaps it was a wish for a utopian world, but it was my dream.

I started my career as a press agent, and shortly after I earned a position as a broadcast journalist covering the daily news in São Paulo. I covered the hard-core events as they occurred. Fires in the favelas - the slums of the city - destroying the homes of hundreds of people. I covered wide-spread floods and the devastation they left in their wake. I covered the abandonment of babies in garbage bins, people dying in public hospitals while waiting to be seen by an overworked doctor and prisoners killed by police officers.

I vividly remember countless people crying in sheer desperation, asking the news crew to help. I also remember countless nights, crying, feeling completely helpless myself.

I interviewed the politicians and decision-makers of my city and country. I covered presidential elections, scandals of corruption and scandals of tax evasion. I came to a sad and harsh realization that there wasn't much that could be done from my position to help improve people's lives. I also witnessed dozens of my colleagues being fired because they asked the wrong question to a politician or didn't cover a story from the acceptable angle.

I started to enjoy international politics and thought that one day I would like to become an international correspondent. For this I needed to master the English language. I had accumulated six weeks of vacation time and decided to use it to help me accomplish that goal. Within a few weeks, I was on a plane to London, England. I had enrolled in an intensive six-week course to learn a language that, currently, I only knew a few basic sentences of.

This was the first time I had set foot outside of my country and the first time I had travelled alone. I had feelings of trepidation and excitement. As soon as I landed, I fell in love with London. I felt like I had been there before; it was like home. I stayed with an English family in the suburbs and travelled on the London Underground during rush hour on my way to school. After school, I explored all the museums and art galleries in the city. I visited every corner of the city that stole my heart, enjoying its parks, concerts, pubs and hidden gems. I was in awe to meet people from all over the world. I spent much of my time studying maps of Europe and planning my next trips. It seemed so easy to travel from place to place, everything seemed so close. Within an hour, I could be in another country.

My time in London was a time of reflection as well as a time of learning and dreaming. I realized that I wasn't satisfied with my life; I wasn't sure what I needed to make that feeling go away. I started to search for something, but I wasn't sure what. I felt restless, uneasy. My life seemed to be on a predictable trajectory. I had a fiancée in Brazil and a promising career, yet I felt unfulfilled. I wanted to explore the world and discover myself and my path. After six weeks, I went back to Brazil with the certainty that I was returning to England.

My plans to return to England had one minor - or major, depending on your perspective - glitch. There was that fiancée. There was a wedding which was already booked. My fiancée, being an established journalist, had lived abroad and travelled extensively when he was younger. He had a successful career and desired to live and work in Brazil, but at that time I had a desire to explore the world. I had a very difficult decision to make, but in the back of my mind I heard my father's wise words. He always encouraged me to follow my dreams and my heart. He was the only person who supported my decision at the time.

I worked really hard for the next six months, saving money. I was determined. The month I was to be getting married, I had a one-way ticket and passport in hand. My mind and heart were set on London: no return in sight.

Upon landing in England at the end of 1995, I had that feeling of homecoming again. Little did I know at that time that this would be the beginning of my journey to self-discovery. I spent a lot of time in contemplation, wondering if I had made the correct decision about leaving my fiancée. He was a good man.

I walked the streets of London asking God or the universe to give me a sign that I had made the right decision, or a sign telling me to go back. My fiancée did not give up on me easily, so that feeling of wondering kept haunting me for months. It was difficult. I felt a push from two sides. One was to go back to a safe, predictable, life, to go back to my job, to the first man I felt in love with. The other was to explore, discover, and dive into the unknown, to get to know myself. It was unpredictable, however. I was craving that change; I wanted to find something else, but I wasn't exactly sure what that something else was.

There were no obvious signs for whether I should stay in London or go back to Brazil. There was, however, a strong feeling, an intuition, that made me stay. My mom sent me a card saying, "When you need to make a decision, make it and don't look back. The moment of absolute certainty will never come." I kept that card by my bedside as a reminder of the decision I had made. From that time on, I started to enjoy the life I was living in London.

Living alone was completely foreign to me. I was used to having my mom do everything for me. I never had to cook, clean or do laundry while living in Brazil. In London, I would work until late at night, then attempt to teach myself how to use a washing machine without ruining my clothing, and to make food that was palatable or at least resembled something that was. All on my own, I had to find a place to live and find a roommate. I also found a job as a waitress to help cover my expenses. Although it was challenging and somewhat scary at first, I loved each moment of my journey; I loved that every decision I made was completely my own. I started to meet people from all over the world who were also in London to learn English. I loved listening to their stories and learning about their traditions, religion and culture. I realized that I had many preconceived, stereotypical ideas of other cultures and their beliefs.

I started to form my own opinion and came to the conclusion that despite our cultural differences, we are all pretty much the same. We all have the same feelings and seek the same things in life. Everyone I met was searching for love, acceptance, education and a career. It was great to experience all of these things in my early twenties; it was what my mom was trying to teach me in Brazil, on a broader scale. I dropped all judgments and criticisms of other people. I could understand the behaviour of others by looking through the lens of their own culture, experience and traditions.

I had a flexible schedule at school which allowed me to travel between the three-month modules. I was able to work at jobs that allowed me to save enough money to travel during my time off from school. This was one of my dreams - the dreams I wrote about in my journal as a girl - coming true. I was able to backpack across Europe and the Middle East. My interest in Middle Eastern affairs was growing, and I decided to volunteer in a kibbutz (a cooperative settlement based on traditional means of agriculture) in Israel, to immerse myself in the world I wanted to learn more about. It was 1999, a year of relative peace in the region. It was there that I started to discover my essence and further define my life's purpose.

My Time in Israel

Summer in the Negev desert. Searing midday heat where a respite isn't even found in the shade. Dry. Burning. It is here, for the first time that I found peace within. The restlessness was replaced with contentment.

The kibbutz that I decided to volunteer at was located in the south of Israel, by the Jordanian border. My work started at four o'clock in the morning to avoid the midday sun. I was working in the fields, in pure contact with nature. My task was to trim the small mango trees that were growing in the sand, due to an advanced irrigation system. I worked alone most of the time, watching the sunrise over the mountains of Jordan in the morning, listening to the birds and feeling the heat of the sun on my skin. The hours were long and quiet. I enjoyed and needed this time alone, reflecting on the purpose of my life.

The desert taught me that happiness comes from within, independent of our outer circumstances, regardless of where we are or what we have. The state of *being* is so much more important than the state of *having*. I started to wonder if the life of financial success that I had been striving for was worth it. I was always looking for instant gratification, but always found that the immediate excitement faded so quickly. Then the empty feeling returned, and the search recommenced.

That lesson was a big realization. I had always thought that the fulfillment and inner peace I so desperately wanted would come from having achieved financial success and a brilliant career. I was truly surprised that at this time when I was volunteering, without money, without fancy clothing, without manicures (Brazilians love their manicures), without a car or career, living in a shared bedroom and eating in a communal dining area, I was happy.

I came to an inner-knowingness that unless my internal state was still and at peace, I could not find a lasting happiness or be satisfied with external circumstances, however wonderful they may be. I felt a huge transformation happening within me during the months spent in the kibbutz; experiencing a simple life and a connection to God. I would still set a goal for financial success, a career and a relationship as long as I managed to maintain my inner state of equanimity. Paulo Coelho, who writes so beautifully, stated in The Alchemist that, "One should let go of the idea that the path will lead you to your goal and the truth is that with each step you take, you arrive." I finally internalized what those words meant.

After the kibbutz, I travelled across Israel, spending most of my time in Jerusalem. I stayed in a hostel within the Old City walls and met many people, who were also in search of their purpose and essence for this life. We would sit on the rooftop of the hostel engaged in philosophical conversations about the meaning of life; the purpose of our very existence.

Jerusalem has such a different energy from the other places I travelled to. A strong energy. Perhaps it is due to the long history of the city, perhaps it is due to the passion and devotion of so many varied beliefs coexisting in such a relatively small geographical space. Here, three of the main religions of the world converge, sharing the very walls that divide them. I watched in awe as the Orthodox Jews walked to the Wailing Wall at the same time as the words of the Quran were echoing in the air, calling the Muslims to prayer, and a priest lead Christian pilgrims along the Via Dolorosa, the route that Jesus walked on the way to his crucifixion, to the stations of the cross. I was amazed to watch all of this occurring simultaneously, understanding the history and devotion of each religion.

Being raised Catholic, there was no mystery about the Christian traditions and sacred sites revered by them. My focus was to learn about and experience that which I did not know. I seized every opportunity to experience the traditions and learn the history of Judaism and Islam. I celebrated the Sabbath in the homes of Orthodox Jews and met many Muslims visiting the Old City. I stopped attending church in my early teens. This time in Israel led me into a deep spirituality, seeking to understand God beyond church walls.

I would wander the streets in the Old City, trying to decide what

I was going to do with my life after I left. The answers did not come, but the process of questioning myself was an important step on the way and it helped me to clarify what I did not want. I no longer wanted to be a person who allowed life to take me where it wished. I did not wish to return to Brazil for the sake that it is where I was born. I did not want to return to broadcast journalism because that is where I previously worked. From then on, I wanted to make conscious choices about my life and existence. I would choose to live a meaningful and purposeful life after leaving Israel; the how would be made clear to me at the appropriate time.

The Article

One afternoon, while walking in the Jewish quarter near the Wailing Wall, I was pondering if I had made a mistake in leaving my fiancée years ago. Every now and then, I had thoughts about him and whether it was an error to leave him. At one time, I believed he was the perfect match for me. I sat on a bench, eating my lunch of hummus, pita and a banana (the easiest and cheapest food) thinking about love. I wondered if people could have love that lasts forever.

Deep in thought, I happened to glance down, and a discarded newspaper written in English stared back at me: "Seek Out Soul Mate, Not Just Life Partner." Even if one doesn't believe in signs, this was pretty hard to ignore. It was a beautifully written article by Rabbi Shmuley Boteach. It poignantly describes love in its true form. The essence of the article is that so many people looking for a relationship view the search as if they were assessing a business partnership: Does the other person match my contributions to the relationship? Boteach suggests that rather than looking for a partner, one should look for a soul mate, someone who you can feel entirely at peace with, share a deep and profound love for, where words are not even necessary to express the adoration you feel for one another. That paper resides in my memory box to this day.

The article made me think of some conversations that I had with a man from the kibbutz named Zelig. He was the one who created the irrigation system in the desert. Every morning he drove the volunteers from the base of the kibbutz to the fields across a main highway, and he returned us each afternoon. I vividly recall the fifteen-minute drive, the moon setting in the early morning hours, the green vegetation, and from the arid sand, the pink flowers blooming, coming to life after the early sun roused them. I loved hearing the owls every morning echoing in the desert. They seemed to beckon to me, speak to my heart and remind me to be true to my dreams. Occasionally, an army Jeep would pass by, breaking my meditative state and reminding me of the tenuous relations between Israel and its neighbours.

Sometimes Zelig and I would engage in conversations about life during our coffee breaks, sitting on the ground under an improvised tent. We spoke of the simplicity of life and of love. He told me that he knew his wife was his soul mate within a few hours of meeting her because she made him laugh. I was surprised that that was all it took for him to know. They had been married for twenty-five years at that point and were about to embark on a world tour for a year. I wondered if I would ever know the certainty that Zelig felt prior to marriage. Would I even want to marry? So many questions. I looked for the answers in the silence of the desert.

Eventually, I felt ready to leave the kibbutz. After Israel, I returned to London to work another six months before moving home. Back in Brazil, I worked at an educational television station producing documentaries and a program to empower entrepreneurs. I thought I was willing to settle in my home country. I thought the feeling of restlessness was gone.

CHAPTER 3
Michael

"Some people only dream of angels. I held one in my arms."
— Author Unknown

I always loved to see the bond between twins. I had gone to elementary school with identical twin sisters. It was a private Catholic school where we had to wear uniforms, so the twins were always dressed alike, adding to the carbon copy effect. The twins switched classes a few times to write each other's exams. They pulled it off many times as the only way to tell them apart was when they were speaking. I always watched them playing together and defending each other when something happened at recess with one of them. As with many sets of twins that I subsequently met, one was more introverted than the other.

When I was in London, I met a Brazilian woman, Mariana, who always told me about her twin sister. She described her with so much love and appreciation. Mariana told me that they were born early. I had no idea what she meant and I never asked. A few months later, her twin sister Juliana was visiting her in London. They were almost identical; the only exception was that one had a beauty mark on her face. They also had different haircuts. Besides those two obvious differences, they were like carbon copies of each other: they spoke the same, they walked the same, even their mannerisms were exactly the same.

They admired each other, they completed each other's sentences and they often spoke to each other without using words. I have always been close to my brother, but I never had the internal and profound bond with him, as twins usually do with one another. Their connection was unique, unlike any other sibling connection. Before the diagnosis, I wondered if my twins would have that strong bond.

On May 15th, 2012, Stel and I drove to Mount Sinai Hospital for my regular prenatal checkup. For the previous five weeks, the drive had become agonizing to me. Every time I went for a checkup, I was given bad news or a warning that our Twin A, Michael, was about to die.

Since we found out about his heart condition, weeks before, every doctor's appointment was just to tell us how his heart was deteriorating. Doctors were now only focusing on our Twin B, discussing how to save my pregnancy instead of finding possible options to save Michael. They had given up on him; my husband gave up on him. I prayed for a miracle, I prayed that our Michael, would prove the doctors wrong. I had read of miracles and heard of many stories where a medical diagnosis had simply been mistaken. My heart and soul prayed that this would be one of those stories. I wanted to save him. I wanted him to live despite the prognosis that if he survived until his birth, he would need three heart surgeries before the age of one and a heart transplant when he was older. Would it be fair to still want him to live? How could I wish the opposite?

In the beginning of my pregnancy it was recommended that I do more genetic tests besides the first trimester screening because of my age - I was 39 years old at the time. Stel and I declined the more invasive procedures knowing that we would accept our children regardless of any diagnosis. A few weeks later, when I was 19 weeks into the pregnancy, we received life altering news. I thought I was going to the hospital to find out the gender of our twins, which happened on the first three minutes of the detailed examination. A couple of hours later, after measuring every bone and every organ, two radiologists walked inside the room and broke the news that Twin A had almost zero chance to survive. I sat wide-eyed, speechless, breathless, looking at the doctors until I looked around the room to meet my husband's eyes sitting on a chair close to the monitor. I burst into tears. Heart condition? Almost no chance to survive? It was agonizing. I never thought a baby could die before its own birth. How could this possibly be happening to us? To me?

We were sent to a genetic counselor that same day and that doctor told us that we could choose to terminate Twin A's life. I couldn't believe what I had just heard. It was too painful for me to even imagine that. I had struggled with infertility for three years and now they were telling me that I could terminate the life of a baby that was given to me. That decision would end the life of Michael and it could cost my entire pregnancy, terminating the life of Twin B, Gabriel, as well.

I was told that if Michael were jeopardizing the life of Gabriel, it would be the best decision. I prayed for a miracle; I prayed that I didn't have to make any decision in regards to Michael's life. It was just too painful. I felt I was in total despair and disbelief that such a thing was happening. How? Why? What had I done wrong?

For a few weeks, I blamed myself. When I first found out that I was expecting twins, I was overwhelmed. I tried to picture how busy my life would be with three little kids. Thomas, my first son, was only two years old at that time. I didn't want to have three kids; I didn't want to drive a mini-van. Yet, there I was with the news of a twin pregnancy; we would grow from a family of three to a family of five in an instant. Some nights I wished, in silence, that it was only one baby. These thoughts haunted me when I was told that Michael was not going to make it. I believed I had created that situation. I was in excruciating emotional pain. I didn't dare share my feelings with anyone. My first feelings of wanting only one baby and then the guilt when I learned about Michael haunted me, daily.

Immediately after a life-changing course that Stel and I attended in Guatemala, I flew to Brazil with Thomas, my first son. I was heading back to the clinic where I had a successful In-Vitro Fertilization, known as IVF, resulting in my first child. I was 120% certain that the next embryo transfer would result in a pregnancy. I felt that I didn't even need to know the result of the pregnancy test twelve days after the transfer, as in my mind, my second pregnancy was already accomplished.

Exactly eight weeks after the course, we found out that it was a twin pregnancy. I immediately focused on what I didn't want: three kids and a busy, hectic life. It was a different feeling from my first pregnancy. I did not take pictures of my belly growing from the beginning, I did not regularly write in my journal. There was a feeling of apprehension. I wasn't happy about the pregnancy… yet. Less than a month after, we were given Michael's diagnosis. How could I not be feeling guilty?

It took me a long time to let the feeling of guilt go. To understand that everything happened had a higher purpose, one that I was yet to discover. Perhaps, my higher self knew and was preparing me for what was to come.

Near the end of April, 2012, a cardiologist at The Hospital for Sick Children, also known as Sick Kids, told us that Michael's heart was very swollen and was covered in fluid. He gave him two more weeks to live. I cried day and night. I couldn't do anything.

I had to hide my feelings from everyone because we chose not to tell anyone about what was happening since the outcome was not definite. I also didn't want to have anyone calling me, requesting updates. The hardest part was that my best friend was preparing a baby shower for my twins. Everyone around us was excited about the twins. I became anti-social because I didn't want to pretend that everything was going well. I needed time and space to be alone and come to terms with what may occur.

At 25 weeks, I was not feeling well anymore. I was very heavy and it was hard to move around. I went for lunch and when I got up from the table, one of my legs was extremely swollen. When Stel came home from work that night, he immediately took me to the hospital. In triage, they told us that I was in premature labour. We were shocked. Among all the scenarios that were given to us, delivering prematurely wasn't one of them. They monitored me all night, administering drugs to accelerate the brain development in the babies and another one to mature their lungs.

While the doctors were monitoring the heartbeats of my twins, at one point they couldn't pick up more than one heartbeat (with the belt that was wrapped around my belly to hear the sound). The signals were on and off. They decided to do an ultrasound instead. What we saw in the monitor was astoundingly beautiful. The twins were touching each other, almost holding hands and their heartbeats were beating at the exact same rhythm for hours. Stel and I could not take our eyes away from the monitor. We watched as Gabriel and Michael were touching hands, moving slightly, but always touching. To this day, I can't believe we didn't take a picture of the monitor. It was incredibly powerful and inspiring. They were supporting each other, caring for each other, giving each other strength.

The hospital managed to stop my labour and I was sent home. I couldn't move much, I wasn't on total bedrest, but I was told to remain as quiet as possible. My mom had come from Brazil to stay with us and celebrate the third birthday of Thomas. I had to tell her what was happening and we cried together. I felt like a scared 10-year-old girl who just wanted to be snuggled by her mom. My mom, however, told me she saw a strong woman in me. She was proud that I dealt with the previous few weeks without completely collapsing. Her kind words encouraged me to keep going, she always has that effect on me.

Two days after I was sent home from the hospital was Mother's Day. I got myself together and we went to a restaurant to celebrate on a beautiful Sunday, the crisp spring air had the slightest promise of the coming warmth. Breathing was extremely difficult. I felt worse than I had ever felt during that pregnancy. I felt as if something had happened. I believe that was the day that Michael had passed away.

The following Tuesday, Stel and I went for my regular checkup at the high-risk pregnancy clinic at Mount Sinai. Part of the checkup was a routine ultrasound; of which I was nearly an expert, by this time. When the technician placed the ultrasound probe on my belly, I saw only one heartbeat. I had seen enough ultrasounds and I knew before she said anything. She choked as she began to say what was obvious to me. I made it easier for her by sharing my observation of only one heartbeat. She told us that she was sorry, and truly she was, her eyes spoke her pain. Then, I burst into tears. That's all I seemed to do those days.

We had known for six weeks that it could happen, but I still expected a miracle. I wanted my son and I wanted him to live. It just wasn't fair. I was so selfish, wanting him to live despite the prospect of multiple surgeries and years spent in hospital. At that point I wasn't thinking clearly. At that point I was a mom who just lost her son. Lost the dreams for her son. I could not celebrate Gabriel because I was in too much pain. I didn't think about Gabriel at all.

My husband hugged me and we cried together. He wanted to be strong for me, but I knew his heart was aching as much as mine. We did not talk about his feelings at the time. I didn't really know how he was coping with it all. All I knew is that we were on this journey together. We drove home in complete silence, both of us lost in our own thoughts. It all seemed so surreal. I felt thankful for the pure love that we had for each other, knowing that it would help us to live through the worst time in our lives.

The unknown was in front of me. Everything I thought I knew was now in question. Everything I had learned seemed to have disappeared. I felt I was in the "space between stories" as Charles Eisenstein, author of *The More Beautiful World Our Hearts Know is Possible*, writes: "The familiar story of the past is crumbling, while the new story has yet to arrive." I kept thinking of his words, paraphrasing them in my mind: "If you find yourself where your old life, or the life that you are used to, is falling apart and your new life has yet to begin, know that you are where you are supposed to be and be comfortable there. At this point it is easy to feel frightened, because of a great unknown in front of you; you need to remain strong while you build your new story, your new life."

The voices of all my other teachers kept coming to my mind the week following Michael's passing. I was told numerous times that we can't unlearn what we've learned. I knew this was a challenge I had to face to keep growing. Growth does not happen just because one decides to grow. It happens as life is experienced. In this case, growth would occur after I grieved, made peace with the situation and moved on to a greater life. For now, I was just a sad mother who lost her son.

The Delivery

It was 7:29pm in the delivery room, there was no cry, just silence. I saw a nurse placing my stillborn baby on a side table to clean him and wrap him in a blanket before being placed in my arms.

At 7:31pm Gabriel was born. Again, no cry, just silence and the rush to take him away to save his life.

I just stared at Michael. I was holding him, a tiny little baby who left us before he even had a chance to live.

I was taken into the observation room and Micheline, a beautiful nurse from labour and delivery, took pictures of us holding Michael. I had not thought of taking pictures. It was awkward. Do we smile? What do we do? Stel stood by my bedside holding Michael, wrapped in the blue hospital blanket.

Micheline came back later, handing me a bracelet she made with Michael's name woven into it. She also gave us the outfit he had been dressed in, so that we could remember. My love goes to the volunteers who knit newborn clothes for babies who do not make it. I had never thought that babies could die so close to their birth. I had heard about miscarriages in early pregnancy, but not about losing a baby closer to term. I felt it was a silence that should be broken.

I had so much pain after the C-section and my emotions were erratic. Other than the pain and intense emotion, my recollection of that time is foggy, at best. It's very strange to deliver two babies under those circumstances. Do I celebrate or do I grieve? What was there to celebrate? I was in deep pain over the loss of Michael.

Four days later, I was discharged from the hospital. They let us see Michael one last time. He had shrunk. He was so tiny and so purple. We said good-bye to our little child. I looked at his tiny face for the last time. Next, we went to the NICU to say bye to Gabriel. I left the hospital in a wheelchair. Empty hands. Broken heart.

Stel and I chose not have a funeral or service for Michael as he had been stillborn. We decided on cremation; to have his ashes in our home where he would be surrounded by our love. When I went to the funeral home to pick up his ashes, I remember being amazed that the ashes were in such a small box. For many months, I did not grieve Michael. I could not. I was emotionally drained.

Every time I thought of Michael, I cried. When I saw twins on the streets or in a park, I felt a stabbing in my heart, so deep that it was ineffable. I thought it could be me pushing a double stroller or running to chase two boys. I longed for something I never had with my baby Michael. I wondered if the pain of losing a child would ever go away.

It took me a couple of years to be able to heal that immense wound inside my heart. I accepted the loss; I accepted the fact that Michael came for a purpose. Perhaps, it was just to support Gabriel for 25 weeks in the womb. Maybe it was to become his protector in this lifetime. When I fully accepted his death, I let go of the pain and I found peace within. I incorporated the loss of Michael into my life. This allowed me to stay focused, allowed me to live in the present moment and celebrate life to its fullest.

Michael will never be forgotten. I still feel his presence; I know he is with us. Stel and I believe that he makes himself visible every time we see a rainbow. I think it's his way to remind us that despite the dark, there is joy, if we look for it.

Every year, to commemorate Michael, our family gathers to release balloons. There are always tears in my eyes as I watch the balloons being carried by the wind. It is as if the balloons retrace the journey of his soul - a few fleeting moments, physically with our family. So easily slipping from our embrace, forever imprinted in our hearts.

CHAPTER 4
Soulmate

*"Important encounters are planned by the souls long before the
bodies see each other."*

– Paulo Coelho

As a student in elementary school, I had to draw, label and colour
maps of different regions, cities and countries. I was always fascinated by the geography and how the maps changed through the
course of history, based on the politics of a region. I had an affini-
ty for maps and studied them carefully. There were a few places in
the world that drew my attention since an early age: Greece, Egypt
and Mesopotamia. I loved learning about the cradle of humanity
and the ancient region is now Iraq, Iran, Syria and Turkey. I co-
loured my maps in brightly, highlighting the Tigris and Euphrates
rivers. In history classes I imagined how life would have been in
the time when the Egyptian pyramids were built. My mind travelled to the Parthenon in Athens, as I learned about Greek Mythology and studied the great Greek philosophers.

In high school, I had a history teacher who taught in such a dramatic manner, as if he had been part of history itself. He trans-
ported my mind to the time of the great political orators in Greece,
I could almost hear Socrates in the Academia. I dreamed about

travelling the world, having a particular interest in that region.

A few years after I graduated from university, I ended up in what I thought was the centre of the world: London. It seemed to be the perfect starting point to go to all the places I had dreamed of. As soon as I arrived, I purchased a map of Europe. It was 1995, the political map of Eastern Europe was changing rapidly. I started to pin the cities I wanted to visit, but after a while there were too many. Instead, I removed all the pins and started to pin the places I had visited. Every time I added a pin I felt a sense of accomplishment, another dream come true.

After eight months in London, I had done some travelling and learned some basic English. Once again, I started to wonder whether I should go back to Brazil or stay longer. I wandered on the streets of London, imagining what I would be missing if I had left. There was so much to explore, literally in the city and figuratively inside my own soul. There was something I could not understand keeping me in Europe.

It was summer. London was always grey, despite the temperature being higher in July and August. Being from Brazil, I craved sunshine, I craved heat, I craved the ocean. Out came The Map, as I fondly referred to it. Where could I go that met all my desires? Greece seemed to be a perfect fit: beaches, heat and sun.

Two days later, one of my classmates and I were flying to Athens. We had a backpack with swimsuits and a travel guide, not much else. No plans were made for the next three weeks. We arrived in

Athens around midnight. Due to the late hour, everything in the city was closed, our only option was to take a taxi to the port. It was a very hot and dry evening. There were dozens of backpackers sleeping on the sidewalk, waiting for the ticket office to open so they could buy ferry tickets to the islands. We had no other option, but to join the queue.

The sun finally appeared and a couple of hours later we were boarding a ferry to Mykonos, where we stayed for one week. Mykonos is a party island; we were immersed in the after-hours nightlife and spending all day on the beach. I was amazed at the navy-blue colour of the ocean and fell in love with Greek food.

Soon it was time to go to the next island: Santorini, the official Greek name being Thira. It is one of the most famous islands in the world, almost a mythical place. There is a strong energy there, perhaps it is from its active volcano or perhaps it is from, as many people believe, a connection to the lost island of Atlantis.

Once again, we boarded an immense ferry. It was so large that it accommodated cars and trucks along with bikes, backpackers and families. We were travelling on a budget, so we got tickets to sit on the top deck, on hard wood benches. One hour into the trip, someone tapped me on the shoulder.

"Excuse me," said the voice, "but are you from Switzerland?" The young men who stood before us were in their twenties. They were Greek-Canadians, we found out later. One of them was named Stelios, who I would come to refer to as Stel.

My English was still a bit broken at that point, but I understood him to be asking if we had a place to stay. Stel offered to negotiate a good rate for us as he spoke Greek and could get us a good deal. My friend and I accepted. We ended up staying at the same hotel and during that week we became friends.

Stel was born and raised in Canada. His parents immigrated from Greece in the late 1960's but his extended family was still living in his ancestral homeland. He was travelling with two friends from university and his best friend from childhood. He had just graduated from optometry school and this trip was a gift from his parents.

Stel's group was fun, or sounded that from what I could understand. He was the loudest of them all and continuously had a big smile on his face. We were just hanging out as travelling buddies for a full week. It was great to discover Santorini through his eyes. He showed me the beauty of Greece that the average tourist doesn't get to see through local hospitality. I learned things about their culture, like how much they enjoy sharing food. Travelling around that island seemed like a movie to me.

There is no lush green vegetation on the island of Santorini, the trees are short and somehow fit in between the famous postcard little white houses that are trimmed in blue. In that arid climate, there are beautiful flowering bushes, grape vines and olive trees. Driving our scooters up and down the hills and around the ocean, my eyes and heart were captured by the breathtaking scenery. Stel took us to places to listen to traditional Greek music and eat authentic, homemade food. I told him how fascinated I had been with Greek history since my childhood and the trip was a very special one for me.

One afternoon, we watched the famous sunset in the scenic Oia, a small town in Santorini, the one headlining many travel brochures to Greece. Stel told me that if the sun touches the sea and it turns red, you would marry the person sitting next to you. I laughed. He had a good sense of humour. I realized he was a great person to travel with.

We said good-bye in Santorini as our groups were destined for different islands. We arranged to meet again in a couple of weeks, in London, when I would be back. Stel and one of his friends were going to have a week-long stopover there, on their way back to Toronto.

London – July 1996

I found a bed and breakfast for Stel and his friend. It was close to the hostel I was living at; both were on Queensway, close to Hyde Park.

By this time, I knew London very well and I took them around the city to sightsee. I showed them the city through my eyes, all the places that tourists wouldn't know about. Stel and I chatted a lot about life that week. There were some misunderstandings, he got lost in translation a few times and I guess I did too. I remember him saying that he was going to write to me. I laughed. Back then, there wasn't email, the internet or text messaging. There were post offices that used stamps on letters, written by hand. His idea sounded sweet, but I doubted he was going to do it.

On his last night, we stopped at Trafalgar Square. It was a nice summer night causing the area to be swarmed with tourists and locals alike. We sat down on the stairs of the National Gallery, then, he kissed me. It was an instant and magical connection. I felt it wasn't the first time it had happened; my soul told me it knew him in another time.

I thought to myself how much time we had wasted that week. In a few hours he was about to leave and I would probably never see him again. We stayed up all night as his train was leaving for the airport around five am. It was hard to say good-bye to him.

Surprisingly, he wrote to me every week for the first few months and then monthly for three years. Our letters were very open, we shared personal stories from the past and what was happening to us in the moment. I kept all his letters. He kept mine.

We got to know each other through the letters. He described the things he liked doing, places he had been, the women he was dating. He sent me pictures of his very first car, he described his days at work and the beginning of his career, his passion to help people. He told me about his friends and his life in Canada. I did the same. Eventually, we started writing about feelings we had for each other. He admired my determination in accomplishing my dreams, by living and studying abroad. He celebrated with me when I was hired for new jobs. I enjoyed the sense of humour in his writing. I sensed his appreciation and zest for life.

I loved receiving his letters. Eventually, they became hand written faxes. Everywhere I went, I sent him postcards, and he did the same. I learned about his passion to discover new places and how much he valued his friendships.

Reading the soulmate article by Rabbi Boteach in Jerusalem, three years after our last meeting, the image of Stel appeared in my mind.

London – July 1999

One month after I read the article, I was back in London. Stel and I were planning to meet again. This time, though, I could speak English and we had deeper conversations about life. He made me laugh the entire time we spent together, walking on the streets of London and on a beautiful boat ride along the Thames River.

At night, we were walking around Trafalgar Square, the very same place we were at, three years before. I had recently watched the movie My Best Friend's Wedding. It's about a woman who realized she was in love with her best friend just before he was set to marry someone else. Years before, they had promised that if they were 28, and not married, they would marry each other. Stel and I said the same thing as a joke, that if we were still single by the age of 30, we would marry each other. I told him that I would only agree to the arrangement if he proposed in front of the National Gallery in Trafalgar Square. He promised. We laughed. Zelig's words ran through my mind: I knew my wife was my soulmate because she made me laugh on our first date.

Time as I knew it collapsed. Our two days together were enough to cement in my heart that he was my soulmate and I fell in love with him, deeper than I thought possible. Our initial meeting on the ferry in Greece was through unusual circumstances, unplanned and unexpected, but as I looked back, I knew it was meant to be. We were now an integral part of each other's lives but living in different parts of the world. We even took a picture on the Greenwich Meridian Line, him standing on one side, and I on the other. It was a metaphor of how we were living at the time: in different hemispheres.

It wasn't about what he could bring into my life, but rather, he had qualities that I didn't. We had a fun, whirlwind visit. Upon his departure, I knew in my soul he was the one. It felt wonderful. The realization that he was the one was overwhelming and electrifying. It was a strange realization. My interpretation of part of the article can be summarized by the following: One should feel fulfilled if you found the soulmate, even if you live on the other side of the world from each other because most people never find it. I kept those words in my head for many years. Living apart from someone you love was a weird concept for me. However, being with Stel at that point wasn't an option because I had never considered moving to Canada; we hadn't even talked about it. We hadn't really spent a lot of time together, either. Besides, I did not wish to live outside Brazil, away from my family for the rest of my life, as I thought I would, in younger days. I had gone to England to learn English and to take some extra courses in media studies to better myself, then began looking into having a more successful career back home. I pictured myself settling back in São Paulo.

I decided it was time to go back to Brazil and continue my career as a broadcast journalist. Two years passed. During that time, we kept in touch, which was easier since technology was more advanced. We sent emails and the phone calls became more frequent.

It was hard for me to be fully present in Brazil; my mind was always thinking about him and what if? However, for a while, I decided to cut our connection. I did not write or respond to his calls for one year.

I made that decision shortly after my grandmother passed away. I couldn't bear the idea of being away from my mom as she was suffering the loss of her mother. I thought about the future when my mom would need me by her side; I wanted to be there for her as she was for my grandma. It was hard to see my mom sad for the first time. She was always so cheerful and positive, qualities she inherited from her mother. I tried to fully live and engage myself in my country.

During our time without communication, Stel had established his life and his career in Toronto as an optometrist. I continued my career in television.

The thought of us being together, however, was still in the back of our minds. After some time without communication, Stel sent me an email saying that I was the love of his life and he did not understand why I was not returning his emails or calls. He informed me that this would be his last email and he wished me a "good life." I tried to reply, but no words came to me. Finally, I called. Hearing his voice, made me want to see him again, once more, even if it was for the last time.

We believed that we were living in a transformative time when it came to our relationship. Deep inside, we were both longing for a different experience than that which we were living, separate from one another.

We knew that fear was stopping us from being together. Fear is the worst thing one can have, because fear is what prevents us from striving for what we want. It's the fear of the unknown, fear of failing. What if it doesn't work?

In July, 2001, we decided that we were going to see each other once more. During that visit we would make a decision, face to face, whether we would continue to be in each other's lives or to move on.

Stel flew to São Paulo on the weekend after 9/11, when the attacks happened in New York City. The world was still in shock about the event and it made me realize that everything in life could change in an instant. We wake up each morning, still alive and life goes on like any other day, but on one day, in one second, everything changes. It did for thousands of people on that day. It had an impact on me.

When Stel arrived, we drove to a farm close to the city, but far enough from distractions, to have a serious conversation. That weekend would be either the last time we saw each other or we would be planning to move forward with our lives, together. My father said that if he was coming all the way from Toronto to São Paulo for the weekend, you knew he was serious. I knew it too. It wasn't hard to make a decision. There was a physical attraction between us, but even more, it was a heart to heart connection.

We spent the weekend at a beautiful historical farm, that used to be a coffee plantation. It had recently been refurbished and turned into a boutique hotel. On the first day, we went on a nature walk, with a guide. There was a very old tree, with an incredible circumference; it would take four to five people to give the tree a hug. The guide mentioned that when you make a wish while hugging the tree, the wish would come true. Stel didn't hesitate and hugged the tree, wishing that I would move in with him.

He does things in a fun way that always makes me laugh. I said yes. There was not much reflection there, I said it as an impulse. I usually made decisions using my analytical mind, but that day was different. I let my heart speak and the decision was made there, under that magnificent centenary tree.

At night, all the guests of that hotel gathered around a campfire. The sky was clear and we could see thousands of stars. A couple of musicians were playing traditional Brazilian country music. The songs had beautiful lyrics, talking about love. Stel did not understand the words, he understood the vibration the music created and we embraced the decision we had made that afternoon.

It was interesting that we had just made a life-changing decision and did not focus on the details of what needed to happen next, the logistics of such a large move. What we did focus on, was a list that Stel had created, to evaluate our values. He wanted to check if our core values were in alignment. They were. We decided to be present and seize the moment, while feeling the love we had for each other.

On the second day, we were each invited to plant a tree. We made it a symbolic act as we dug the hole to plant the small tree. We said that time would tell how well the tree and our relationship would grow: if one flourished, the other would as well. Stel left after the weekend and I had quite a bit of planning to do.

I talked to my parents first; they supported me in my decision. I told my mom that I would stay if she asked me to. She said to go, that I had to follow my heart. I knew deep down in her heart, she did not want me to be away from her and my dad. I knew how much she would miss having me around to do the things we used to do together. However, we both knew that my parents would visit us in Canada. They had visited me in London and Israel and we travelled together to many other places in Europe and North America. This was another step in my mom fulfilling her dreams of travel.

Months passed. Stel and I were communicating daily, making plans. I flew to Toronto for the weekend to meet his parents and get to know the city a little more.

I finished my master's degree, quit my job and I told my friends and extended family of my plans to move to Canada while Stel started to shop for houses. Taking a huge leap of faith, a few months later I landed in Toronto, this time it would be my permanent home.

Starting together

I knew what was involved in being a foreigner, an immigrant to a new country after living in London for a few years. In Toronto, I would have to face a new marketplace, overcome my fear of approaching people for jobs with my accent, start my career over, learn about a new culture, and make new friends: build a new life. I calculated the risks and I was willing to give it a chance because I believed in the love between Stel and myself. We knew there would be obstacles to overcome, but we saw no barriers between us.

On my 30th birthday, I had been in Canada for 30 days. Stel invited our families out for dinner to celebrate these two milestones with us. It was a meaningful birthday, with both sets of parents present. My parents had come to Canada to celebrate with me. My brother, sister-in-law and some friends also came out for the event. When we arrived back home that night, Stel had prepared a surprise for me in the basement of our first house. He had printed an oversize photo of Trafalgar Square and right there he proposed to me. I had no idea what had just happened, and I did not answer as I was totally at a loss for words. This dramatic event was something new to me, in Brazil we don't have a tradition of giving a ring at a formal proposal. It was incredible. He said that because we couldn't go to Trafalgar Square, he brought it to me. He is incredibly creative and original to this day. Eventually, I was able to find words and accepted his proposal.

Sixteen months later, we got married.

It was a rough beginning.

Even though we knew each other for seven years, we had never dated like most couples. We had only spent 45 days with each other. We saw each other on long weekends, expensive weekends. We would fly from Toronto to São Paulo, or from São Paulo to Toronto. Sometimes to New York or Rio de Janeiro; three or four days here and there. Only a couple of people knew about our trips. We were both trying to carry on with our lives in our own countries but we both felt awakened since our re-encounter in London. It was as if we had been put together for a purpose. We tried to be with other people in the meantime, but every time a new email showed up in our mailboxes the desire to be together became even stronger.

Living together under one roof, we had to figure out not only the small, daily things that affect all couples, but also the more meaningful and profound issues. Needless to say, the first couple of years were tough. Those years brought an awareness within both of us that challenged us to question how we could foster the growth in our relationship, and also in ourselves.

At first, we took the traditional route of marriage counselling. This was great as it led us to a path of self-awareness, pointing out root causes for our actions and decisions. We had to dive into a big hole, a very uncomfortable place to be. For the longest time, a lot of the discussions from counselling became ammunition for our arguments. We became emotionally drained and exhausted. We argued about everything, the small things and the more important decisions of life. There were arguments over things like putting the clothes in the laundry basket to the most important values: family traditions, culture, naming the kids we didn't have. I questioned myself several times. What was the purpose of the marriage? Why did I insist on staying when it was so difficult? Why hadn't Stel put all of these things on his list of values that we had to agree on?

Throughout all the trying times, we knew our love was greater than the arguments and bickering, that there was a sense of sacredness to it. We never tried to compete with each other or pretend to be someone we were not, just to please the other person. I always loved his uniqueness and his authenticity. There was always a sense of completion when we were together.

He supported me every step of the way while I was adjusting to the Canadian lifestyle. Getting my first job here was tough. Despite a master's degree and years of experience in broadcasting, I did not have Canadian experience in the workplace and English was my second language. Through the ups and downs of the job search, Stel always encouraged me to keep going. He became my rock, cheering me up every time I heard a no. He was the one who also celebrated the day I came home from a job interview and announced that I had been hired by a local television station. It wasn't a glamorous position, but he made me feel I had just been offered the job of a news anchor for a major national network. It was things like that which made me believe we could find a way to sort out our challenges and live with our differences.

Two years after getting married and many hours of counselling, we each committed to a journey of self-discovery, together. That was the beginning, laying an important foundation in our relationship. Most importantly this stopped us from blaming the other, helping to lead us to become fully aware of our own personal choices and actions. I learned how to reflect on my own attitudes, without judgment. That change created a more meaningful relationship as I learned to recognize what was keeping me stuck and perpetuating the same problems in my life. Achieving personal growth is a constant work in progress that we committed to pursue.

As life went on, there were still issues that needed work, such as choosing the names of our children. That was a particularly sensitive issue. In the Greek tradition, the children are named after the grandparents first name. From the beginning, I told Stel that I did not agree with it. I was raised with a brother who was named after my father. My brother never accepted his name and had an identity issue growing up. I wanted my kids to develop their own identities without carrying the weight of a name that had its own history. Stel stood up for his tradition and we argued over this for a long time. It kept me awake many nights and cost me a lot of tears. It was hard for him too, if he agreed with me, he would have to go against the wishes of his parents and generations of tradition.

The issue of naming our children caused great tension between us for years. We tried different approaches to come to terms with it, but all of them ended up in arguments. It was the hardest thing to deal with. We finally reached a compromise by using his father's first name as the middle name for our first son, Thomas.

This decision still created animosity with his parents, but eventually that too got resolved. There are things in life that we only learn with maturity, with inner growth and with experience. Looking back, I had a lot of ego involved in those arguments. It could have been simpler if I had known that at the time.

I discovered that working on myself was the secret to keeping a healthy and fulfilled relationship. That became the most powerful tool to embrace as a couple. With unconditional love between us, we were ready to face the challenges that were about to arise.

CHAPTER 5
Infertility

"When you believe in a thing, believe in it all the way, implicitly and unquestionable."

— *Walt Disney*

When you really, really want something, you become focused on it and see nothing else. I didn't see food at the grocery store, I saw mothers with their giggling and gurgling infants in shopping carts and strollers. I didn't see the people walking on the street, I saw only the children playing. I saw mothers wiping faces, teaching lessons, kissing bruised knees, everywhere I went.

I started to dread checking the mail as it seemed that all I received were baby shower invitations. My closest friends were happily announcing their pregnancies and due dates. There were ten showers in just one year. The inevitable question was asked to me as well. When was I planning to start a family? How do you answer that question? I started wanting to ask people for a manual with specific instructions on how to accomplish this goal, just to be sarcastic. However, that wasn't my personality. I was frustrated, I wanted to announce that I was expecting, I wanted to hold my own baby. Many people told me that I should just relax and I would get pregnant. Only people who had never faced infertility could say that because they decided to have a baby, had sex and got pregnant. Easy.

After a year of attempting to conceive without any success, I was referred to a fertility clinic. I had been diagnosed with *unexplained infertility*. I was started on the conventional treatments for infertility. This included taking mild doses of hormones, closely monitoring my cycles as well as daily ultrasounds and blood tests.

The hormones were prescribed to stimulate the uterus, producing more follicles which could become eggs. The advice the doctor told me was to relax and have plenty of sex. I remember having to schedule 'sex' in my husband's calendar, placing it after a lunch with a client and before an afternoon appointment with the accountant. Sex became a job, a routine, a task to be accomplished. This is never a place where one feels relaxed or sexy.

Even going to the fertility clinic became part of my routine. There is no dignity or privacy when undergoing fertility treatments. Eventually, I didn't care if there was one or ten people in the ultrasound room. I developed an attitude of whatever, exposing what was just another part of my body. Month after month there were more hormones, ultrasounds, scheduled sex appointments, tests, and eventually negative results. Again, who could remain relaxed in this situation?

At the clinic, I saw many couples facing infertility. Dozens of women marched into the clinic every morning. They were there, just like me, monitoring their cycles, having blood tests and ultrasounds. We saw each other every morning for months at a time, only acknowledging the others with a nod. We knew nothing of anyone else, not even names, yet there was an innate connection because we were sharing the same trials. Some women became engrossed in magazines while waiting, some worked on their laptops. I could only stare at the walls, where hundreds of baby photos stared back at me. I assumed these were photos of babies that were made by this clinic.

As the months passed without any results, the treatments became more aggressive and sometimes uncomfortable. The hormones became stronger, creating drastic and fluctuating moods. One moment I would be calm, the next I would be laughing, then immediately transition into crying without justification. Stel coped extremely well with all of the changing emotions and personalities he had to face each day. He was even able to inject me each morning, while enduring the evil eye I gave him. I had tried to inject myself once, but with a fear of needles I couldn't even pick one up, much less inject it into my stomach.

I decided to make my infertility and the treatments I was undergoing public, by writing a blog to document and share my experiences. Immediately, I was bombarded with emails from women who were living and had lived the exact same experience as me, that said they had been too embarrassed to talk about it; ashamed and guilty that they couldn't become pregnant.

Making it public was liberating; it took a lot of pressure off of me. I no longer had to answer the dreaded question about when I would start my own family and the constant reminders that I wasn't "getting any younger." Not only did making the journey public normalize it for me, but it also made other women realize that they weren't the only ones facing similar frustrations, embarrassments and a whole other range of emotions. It was a healing process for everyone involved.

I tried to stay positive, happy and as distracted as I could by studying, working, meeting with friends and practicing yoga. Still, some days I felt discouraged and sad. These were the days when I loved my husband most and when I finally understood what Zelig meant when he explained the value of having a spouse who could make you laugh. Stel was always able to pull me out of a low mood. He was the husband at the clinic who made jokes and kissed his boys before he handed the jar to a nurse who sent them to be processed in a lab.

I believed in my heart I was going to be a mom and he was the one who reminded me that it was a matter of when, not a matter of *if*, I got pregnant. He continued to be my rock.

Day twelve. The day I dreaded, yet anxiously awaited. Day twelve was the day that, at eight am, I had the definitive blood test for that month. The four longest hours of my life were the hours from the blood test to noon, when I received the phone call letting me know if the embryo had implanted; if I was pregnant. Answering that call was almost painful, as month after month, the result was the same: negative. Stel, however, knew that one day he would be able to pop the champagne waiting in our fridge.

I lost ground with each negative result. Only the belief that I would someday hold my own baby and my husband's love kept me going. My instinct led me to explore alternative therapies. The fertility clinic was only addressing the physical aspect of the unexplained infertility; I felt there were deeper levels to the *unexplained* part of the problem.

After my road of self-discovery in Israel, I continued to enroll in courses that furthered my understanding of the self. During one such course, I met a naturopathic doctor from Alberta who was also enrolled in the course. Christian and I became friends. It was Christian that suggested that the infertility may be rooted in my emotions; issues that were so deep and powerful, that they kept me from becoming pregnant. This made sense to me as there was not a physical explanation - from Stel or myself - that would keep me from having children.

From Christian, I learned or perhaps remembered from somewhere deep inside my being, that our emotions, mind, body and spirit are all one. I started to learn about the holistic body and how to integrate all four bodies into one unified person. I wanted to restore the inner peace that I had felt while pruning mango trees growing in sand, under the desert sun.

I continued treatments at the fertility clinic, which were now more invasive, while I learned more about other options. The clinic was attempting in-vitro fertilization. This is where mature eggs are retrieved from a woman, fertilized in a lab and transferred back to the uterus as an embryo. These cycles were a disaster, not only were they painful but also left me physically exhausted and emotionally devastated. Most of the embryos did not meet certain quality criteria or didn't survive or didn't grow to the blastocyst stage (when they reach five days in lab and are then ready to be transferred). There were very few that were of a high enough quality, indicating that they could be transferred.

After one such cycle, I went to complete a ten-day detox with Christian at his clinic in Canmore, Alberta. The detox included a four-hour hike up a mountain. At the bottom of the mountain, there was a sign with a warning about bears and wolves in the area. I wish I had overlooked that sign. My mind could focus on nothing but fear of the bear that never appeared, for the entire ascent into the Canadian Rockies. At the peak, in the middle of the clouds and standing on a precipice, Christian likened my journey of infertility to the climb we just made. He patiently explained that much like the hike, where I was fearful and focused on what I did not want – a bear attack – my journey to pregnancy was the same. He convinced me that I had to let go and enjoy the process, rather than focusing on the final result.

The climb down was entirely different. I released the fear of a bear attack, choosing to replace that fear with a surety of safety. Only then, did I begin to revel in the nature that surrounded me. I saw the vegetation that was unique to this elevation and latitude, I smelled the wild flowers and breathed the crisp air. All of this beauty was there on the ascent, but my fear blinded me from its presence.

The experience left me profoundly changed. That little walk up a mountain left me with an understanding that whatever beliefs I had, must be replaced with new ones. Rather than fear-based beliefs that limited me, I would choose to have and embrace beliefs that empowered me, helping me on the road to my goals. I felt a sureness, a calm, that I hadn't felt before, *knowing* that I would have a baby of my own.

After one last embryo transfer in Toronto that had a negative result, I was told that my eggs were not good and to consider an egg donor. This left me in shock; there was never a discussion of this at any previous appointment. Why had I undergone all of the previous treatments, the pain and the trauma to my body, mind and soul if, in fact, my eggs were *not good*. In that instant, I felt broken in every sense.

My husband lives in a state where he knows everything is possible, he always finds a way to accomplish what he seeks. One morning, he woke up very early, put on his running shoes and literally ran to the fertility clinic. Upon arriving, he asked them for our files without giving further explanation. He was done with them. He had enough of seeing my pain and sharing the disappointment of negative test results every four weeks over the course of three years. When he returned with our files, he told me to pack my bags. We knew of a fertility clinic in São Paulo, that treated a cousin of mine, where women were seen in a holistic manner. We decided this was an avenue worth pursuing.

Applying what I had learned from Christian and the mountain, I decided to enjoy every moment of my trip to Brazil, not just the final moment we were hoping for. I was going to be treated at a clinic that held a similar philosophy to that which I was learning and I would be able to spend time with my family and friends.

"One day you are going to understand why this is happening to you." That is what one of the doctors from the holistic clinic in Brazil said to me during our first meeting. I was astonished to hear those words uttered by a doctor. I was used to the pragmatic, scientifically-minded doctors that I had known up until then. Doctor Edson and his team were different. He was the head of the clinic and very caring and compassionate. He was concerned about my well-being after three years of stressful treatments. I saw a psychologist and nutritionist at his clinic. He approached my treatment from many angles. Not only did he have me start taking hormones and nutritional supplements, but also had me focus on finding and maintaining emotional stability: happiness, regardless of the situation.

The time I spent in São Paulo for my treatments ended up being the most fun I had in years. I was out every night, laughing and reminiscing with my friends about our days. I spent hours talking with my family, sharing meals and loving the feeling of being close to those I love most.

I was learning how to monitor my thoughts. This process would help dissolve any residual negative energy from my past. I stayed focused and present, observing my emotions, without judgment. This was a powerful process that helped to transform my situation, accepting what is. It was a magical transformation, aided by being in my home country surrounded by those who knew me longest. The first attempt at the new clinic proved to be the best cycle I had in over three years. Everything is counted in cycles during fertility treatments: how many eggs, how many embryos, the quality of each. I kept in mind that all I needed was one, one viable embryo to implant. This cycle, I had nine.

The ominous Day 12 arrived. However, this Day 12 had a different vibe about it; perhaps it was the power of my monitored thoughts, perhaps it was because my mom was with me. As I had done for years, I showed up at the clinic to have my HCG (Human Chorionic Gonadotropin) levels measured. This is the hormone that is produced when a woman is pregnant. While we waited the four hours for the results, we spent time at a shopping mall, then headed home just before noon. It seemed that every relative we had was calling, and each time the phone rang my heart raced.
In an attempt to keep my mind occupied, I turned on the TV and started watching the Olympics in Beijing. The track and field events were being televised when the clinic called. With cold, sweaty palms I answered. The receptionist asked me to hold for Dr. Edson. I don't recall any words that he told me, other than "It's positive." I screamed at the top of my lungs and burst into tears. This was the exact moment I had dreamed about for years. I was finally pregnant!

Santiago, the main character in Paulo Coelho's *The Alchemist* says, "When you want something, all the universe conspires in helping you to achieve it." I always believed that. I always believed in the power of dreams.

When I learned to set goals, well defined goals, with emotional charge, I literally watched my life unfold. I watched in awe at the materialization of all that I had planned. Napoleon Hill wrote, "Goals are dreams with a deadline." I believe that they are truly magical when you add Hill's concept of "burning desire" to make them a reality and work towards achieving them with a timeline in mind. Many times, I heard people saying that they didn't achieve the goals by the date they had planned, that the goals seemed too far away as the date approached. I had been there many times too, but each time I failed in achieving a goal, I saw it as an incredible opportunity to re-evaluate the action I took toward my goal and the events that subsequently occurred.

My teacher Gina Mollicone-Long explains in her book *Think or Sink*, that there aren't failures in life, just feedback. If we keep that in mind, we can set new goals, being flexible with timelines, and watch to see how the goal we set shows up.

Many times, when we have a dream or set a goal, we are tested. It feels like the universe tests everything we have learned along the way. This is the point when many people give up because the lessons are hard, and at times the challenges are painful. I believe that it is at that point - the point when we persevere - the magic happens and the dream or goal comes into existence.

I did not give up on my dream to be a mom. It was a long and challenging road, a trying road. A road full of lessons, with the most important one being: to hold steady to my belief, regardless of the challenges.

Nine months and ten days after that phone call, my first son, Thomas, was born.

CHAPTER 6
Before the Storm

"Give me six hours to chop down a tree and I will spend the first four sharpening the axe."

– Abraham Lincoln

I realized that every event and situation that occurred up to this point was all a preparation, an education. I would draw on all the lessons I had learned and strength I had accumulated to allow me to live up to what I was about to face.

Two years had passed since the birth of my first miracle. He was growing and thriving. Every day it astounded me that I loved him more than the previous day. Watching him grow, learn and change was gratifying for Stel and myself. We were the image of a family that I had always envisioned.

Through the years, Stel and I always had the goal to continue to evolve individually as well as grow as a couple and a family. He supported me when I decided to leave my career as a journalist, pursuing an avenue that could make a greater difference in people's lives. I decided to switch careers. I had never considered putting my years earning my degrees, aside. I knew the knowledge I had gained would always be with me and at this point in my life

I had a greater calling. My new career as a life coach was to help women to rediscover their greatness; to support them in creating and living a more fulfilled life. Not only had I studied the theory, but I lived the principles. I also continued to volunteer at various organizations, fundraising for different charities.

Part of the evolution of our family was to attempt to have another child. Stel and I had decided that it felt like the right time to welcome another life, a sibling for Thomas, into our home and our hearts. Before embarking on that journey, we took some time for ourselves, to further our evolution as individuals.

Guatemala
November, 2011

The rainforest was dense; the air was thick. Fog obscured the tops of the trees and the path we were walking from our room to the restaurant. Howler monkeys echoed through the forest and the fog, seemingly as loud as dinosaurs. Stel and I had been attending an intensive course in Guatemala, for the past two weeks. People had flown from all over the world, converging in this humid paradise, to discover the answers about humanity's very existence. We all shared the awareness that living a fulfilling life was more than just accumulating material wealth. We wanted to delve inside our beings, to slow down, to find answers: to learn.

We learned that we had to focus, with intensity, on what we wanted. I was laser-focused on having another child. That course brought together all the ideas and principles that Stel and I had been studying for the last ten years: laws of attraction, manifestation, laws of life, projections, consciousness and unconsciousness and quantum physics.

In Guatemala, we learned different approaches to transform our thinking into something multifaceted. We discovered unconscious patterns of behaviour that did not support us, and by bringing those patterns into our consciousness, we would be able to be aware of them, allowing us to make the necessary shift toward our own evolution.

Each morning I would write for hours, contemplating the nature in front of me. I wrote until I felt empty. We used this exercise to cast away any thoughts or beliefs that no longer served us and to awaken the knowledge and power each of us had.

I felt a profound transformation occurring within me while attending the course. I made a concerted effort not to revert to old patterns of thought and behaviour; I was ready to take on that challenge and take my life to the next level where I would be more confident and empowered.

I was open to change and I understood that personal development is all about change. Our teachers taught us that only when we really desire change and are ready for it, we could develop the mechanisms that would allow us to follow through on the change we needed and wanted. If we could stay true to that goal, regardless of the challenges placed in front of us, we would move to the next level.

At the end of the two weeks, I knew that if I had thoughts that didn't support me or if I wasn't 100% focused on what I wanted, I would be tested.

The last three days of the retreat, we travelled to Tikal National Park, one of the major sites of the Mayan Civilization. Benedicto, our guide and a Mayan descendent, was as charismatic as he was knowledgeable. He taught us an in-depth, true history of the Mayan people as well as their spiritual traditions. Many of the tourists asked about the 2012 Mayan prophecy; he reassuringly told them that it simply meant the end of one cycle of time and the beginning of another. He went on to explain that as in any time of transition, turbulence may occur in individuals' lives as well as in humanity as a whole.

In my broken Spanish, I asked him questions about the Mayan ceremonies and beliefs. Our conversations went well into the night. I was in awe to learn about their level of spirituality, their mythology and sacrifices as well as how they had mastered acoustics, astronomy and architecture.

Without knowing our story or that we had decided to try to have another child, Benedicto took Stel and I aside one afternoon. He brought us through the forest, to a recent excavation of a Mayan fertility goddess. My heart stopped and I gasped as he said "This is where women who were trying to get pregnant would come." He explained that in the past, the Mayan women would make offerings and pray to have children at this very spot.

My eyes were transfixed on the ancient statue of Ixchel. As she stared back at me, I knew, with certainty, that I would be a mom for the second time. Peace washed over me. I felt a sense of calm, I was in balance with my inner self, a feeling I had not felt so strongly since my time on the kibbutz in Israel.

Two weeks after our encounter with the Mayan fertility goddess, Thomas and I were on a plane to Brazil. We arrived in São Paulo in early December, an exciting time as Christmas and New Years' celebrations were being prepared. Stel had to stay in Canada to attend to his business, but would be joining us for the holidays.

It felt like a homecoming, to be back at the fertility clinic. Stel and I had chosen to have some of our embryos frozen, almost three years earlier. It felt like the right time for a second pregnancy. My mother accompanied me; we were both in a positive state of mind. Seeing so many photos of babies and their parents on the walls of the reception area almost brought me to tears. There was a certainty in me as I waited. I didn't believe, I knew, I would have a successful IVF cycle and become a mother again.

My name was called and I was led to Dr. Edson's office. He was happy to see me again and thrilled at my progress as a person and my role as a mother. He must have sensed the growth that had taken place in me since he first met me. He asked me a question that I didn't expect. He wanted to know if I wished to have one or two embryos transferred. He told me that the chances of having a multiple pregnancy was high because of advancements in technology and the quality of my embryos. With Stel being in Canada, I was faced with making this decision, alone.

I had made important and life-altering decisions before. Leaving Brazil at a young age, breaking my engagement, leaving my career as a journalist were all monumental choices that I had made, all by myself. I had taken time with each of those choices and measured the pros and cons of each. This decision that I was asked to make didn't come with the luxury of time. Without fully considering all the possible implications and consequences, I said to Dr. Edson, "I came all the way from Canada. We might as well transfer two, to maximize my chances." He agreed and very calmly replied that he would do the two transfers, aiming for a single pregnancy. At the time, I had no idea why he said that.

Twelve days after the embryo transfer, Dr. Edson called to tell me that I was pregnant, with HCG levels of 127. The level was similar to the level I had at the beginning of the pregnancy for Thomas, so I assumed that only one embryo implanted. I was to return to the clinic prior to leaving for Canada in mid-January.

Stel had arrived just after learning the news. We all journeyed to my parent's country house for the holidays, overjoyed. My family and I were excited about the year ahead; with a new baby arriving we all felt good vibrations. I recall conversations about more presents under the tree and how our dining table would be growing again.

Before travelling back to Canada, I had an ultrasound at Dr. Edson's clinic. I went alone as Stel had already left and my mom was watching Thomas. At the clinic, the technician turned the monitor so I could see, she placed the probe on my stomach and then I saw it: two sacs. I thought she had gone too fast for me to see clearly, however, having hundreds of ultrasounds in the past five years, I recognized what the monitor showed. She confirmed that there were two and without hesitation, said that they were OK.

Upstairs in his office, Dr. Edson had already seen the results. I didn't know what to say. I was in shock. The fertility goddess must have felt accomplished, I thought to myself, as I held the ultrasound photos.

On the phone call to Stel, after the appointment, we joked that we had not been specific enough when setting our goal of another pregnancy.

Chapter 7
Unwelcome Journey

"The road might be long. The journey might be challenging and full of dangers. Take a rest, if you must, but never turn back. Your very next step can be your moment of triumph. Your very next battle can be your greatest victory."

— *Dr. Bohdi Sanders*

I walked into the NICU two days after I gave birth to Michael and Gabriel. Stel had left for the day, but my friend Renata was there with me. I asked her to help me out of bed and into a wheelchair. I was too weak to walk from 7-south to the NICU.

Renata had seen Gabriel a few hours before and tried to help me visualize how small he was. I had very little recollection of seeing him two days prior. My memory of seeing him then was hazy, at best. I had no concept what a baby weighing 900 grams (two pounds) looked like. All the babies I had ever seen had been plump and healthy, sometimes weighing almost ten pounds at birth.

Not having the energy or desire to change, I was still wearing the blue hospital gown as Renata wheeled me through that wing of the hospital to the NICU. The last time I saw those corridors I was being rushed into the operating room. This time was a slower ride; it seemed so long.

Finally there, we had to wash our hands in a long, deep stainless steel sink, with surgical strength soap, then use alcohol gel before requesting to enter. I told the nurse that I was the mother of Gabriel, in bed 25. We had to wait. I had no concept of time again, we could have waited a few seconds, a few minutes. At last, we were allowed to enter. Everything seemed foggy.

As the doors to the NICU opened, I began an unwelcome journey. A friend likened it to purchasing a ticket to a roller coaster ride that had no end; perpetual inclines, drops and gut-wrenching loops.

The NICU was a large room, filled with incubators, side-by-side. There was too much information to take in; machines, oxygen cylinders, tubing, scary looking contraptions. Nurses were walking around and there were a few mothers sitting by the bedside of their tiny babies. I didn't know where to look. It was busy and loud, not the quiet nursery for premature babies that I had imagined. Beeping machines and alarms seemed to be everywhere, chiming off without a single point of origin; it was all around. I was overwhelmed.

The unit, at first sight, seemed to be a much bigger place than it actually was. Renata knew where to take me. She turned right and then left. Sitting in a wheelchair, I was at eye-level to the babies laying inside the incubators and the signs that indicated the name, date of birth and weight of each baby. Pink signs for girls and blue for boys. I could see their miniature feet, rolled blankets keeping their legs contained.

The blue sign appeared. "Twin B, Gabriel – 26 weeks + 1 day, 900 grams." My living baby, inside the incubator, so small and frail. I was in shock and in disbelief. I felt dizzy. I thought I was going to faint, the piercing odour of the alcohol sanitizing gel adding to the effect. I wanted to scream, but the scream was stuck in my throat. Everything in this place was surreal. Does the world even know that such a place exists? I didn't, until that moment. How can a baby survive at 26 weeks gestation outside of the mother? How could a baby as tiny as 900 grams live? A life, a soul, a world of possibilities contained within 900 grams.

Initially, I mentally collapsed into an abyss where reality faded. A darkness rose around me, enveloping me. I felt I had been sucked into a vortex, my breath was gone, escaping me and I couldn't inhale. I was without words, without thought. I closed my eyes, hoping that when I opened them, my world would return to its normal state of being.

It didn't work. I was still there. It was real. This was my new reality.

I was watching Gabriel while a nurse was talking to me. When I looked at her, I saw her lips moving, but I couldn't hear her words. Gabriel was laying inside an incubator, its walls full of condensation because the temperature inside had to be kept high as he could not regulate his own body temperature yet. I did not see a baby, I saw wires, monitors and a breathing machine that was larger than his tiny face. His vulnerable body was covered with thin hair, his fragile skin was purple and he had an IV in one of his miniscule arms. His eyes were still fused. My baby was so small, the equipment around him so big and terrifying.

There wasn't anything in the NICU that made one think it could be a nursery. Absent from this unit were cribs, fluffy blankets, teddy bears and baby décor. It was a sterile place, lacking any resemblance of where new babies are joyously welcomed into the world. To me, at that moment, the NICU was a place where all the dreams of a new parent were smashed, taken away in a mere instant.

That first visit to the NICU, of which I recall very little, only lasted a few minutes. If I was able to think at that moment, I could not have predicted what was to come. Both my son and I were in survival mode. Nothing more.

Later that day, while I was in my room, a doctor came to give me an update on Gabriel. He was standing in front of the hospital bed. I don't remember his name, but I remember his face and his words. He told me that my son had PDA, patent ductus arteriosus, which is a persistent opening between two major blood vessels leading from the heart. The opening, called the ductus arteriosus, is a normal part of a baby's circulatory system before birth, usually closing shortly after. In Gabriel's case, it was still open. This meant that Gabriel had a heart condition. That was where I stopped listening: a heart condition. Yet he kept speaking. Everything else he said sounded like someone speaking under water, in very slow motion. I cried uncontrollably. He asked me why I was crying.

The words that came to my mind to yell at this bloody automaton would have probably had me kicked out of the hospital, or at the very least placed me in a very different kind of ward. Was it possible that a human being could not understand the pain and turmoil I had lived through for the last six weeks and that I could not handle more bad news? Did Gabriel's medical file not state that he had just lost his twin due to a heart condition? Could this man not comprehend the terror that a mother feels at the idea of losing another child?

I thought I had shut down before. This was a whole new level of shutting down. I called Stel, who immediately returned to the hospital. I asked him to speak with the doctors. I had nothing left. The coping strategy that worked for me in the beginning was to avoid listening to anything about Gabriel's health. In my mind, Gabriel only had to stay in the NICU until he gained enough weight to go home. I had no idea about the complexities that a child of premature birth could face.

On the third day, Thomas came to visit his brother. I was happy to see him. I missed having him around, talking to his baby brothers in my belly. We all entered the NICU together. I was still in a wheelchair, being too weak and in too much pain to walk.

The first time Thomas saw his brother, he was under special lights because of jaundice, a common condition in newborns. He looked purple. His eyes were covered. He was getting a blood transfusion and because he was breathing with a CPAP machine, a mask covered most of his face.

CPAP stands for Continuous Positive Airway Pressure. The baby does all the breathing, but the machine helps tc keep the lungs open in between breaths.

"He's chocolate," Thomas said. I cried while trying to make the situation as normal as possible for him. He didn't know any different. He was just three years old; we only answered the questions that he posed.

During my pregnancy, the high-risk clinic advised me about how to talk to Thomas about Michael. I hadn't even considered telling him about his stillborn brother. A nurse at the antenatal clinic, told us we would need to have age-appropriate answers ready for when Thomas asked. She was right. A soon as we left the NICU, Thomas asked when his baby sister was going to arrive. Throughout my pregnancy, he told me that he was positive that he was going to have one sister and one brother. My heart stopped. I froze. I could not answer him.

Stel took him out for lunch that afternoon and at the restaurant, Thomas asked again. Stel told him that baby Michael wasn't going to stay here with us, that his job would be to look after us from up there. He was content with the answer for that moment, but kept asking me the same question. It was a complicated question to answer. He was trying to make sense of what happened, but how could I explain to him when I didn't even understand it myself?

Four days after the delivery, I was ready to be discharged. This is when Stel and I said our last goodbyes to Michael.

On the elevators down, there was a family carrying a car seat with their newborn baby. I had also just given birth, yet I was leaving the hospital empty-handed and with a broken heart.

At the back of the hospital – at the Murray Street exit – there is a revolving door. With the feeling of an empty heart, I began to visualize the day I was going to be carrying Gabriel out those doors in his car seat. I held that vision each day when I left the hospital. I felt the emotions of carrying the car seat, I saw our family together, exiting through those revolving doors… and I did that every day for 146 days.

Home

One more time, Stel and I drove in complete silence. It was a beautiful spring day. People were outside, enjoying the weather. I saw college students riding their bikes, new mothers pushing their strollers and men in suits rushing along. It surprised me that the world continued, people were still living. My world had collapsed; time had stopped for me. I wondered how I would carry on.

Arriving home, my friend Luciana was delivering food for me. She was at a loss for words and I couldn't stop crying. I also didn't know what to say. Are there really any words to describe how I felt? My mom was also there, she hugged me. There are some moments in life when words would only be a hindrance. In these moments, all that is ineffable is spoken through the heart and eyes.

Stel sent an e-mail to all of our family and friends to share the details about the birth of the twins.

Dear family and friends,

"If you concentrate on finding whatever is good in every situation, you will discover that your life will suddenly be filled with gratitude, a feeling that nurtures the soul."
-Harold Kushner

Fabi and I will first say that we are excited to announce that we are parents again to a healthy boy named Gabriel who was born on May 17, 2012 at 7:31pm.

Out little angel Michael unfortunately did not make it due to a heart defect. We know for sure there is a huge purpose to the love that we share with him and we always say everything happens for a reason and we have an idea what it is, but only time will tell.

We are super proud parents and we want you guys to focus on the fact that there will be Thomas and his brother running around and we also know that little Michael will always be with us.

You are all incredible people and we are grateful to have all of you in our lives and our family's life.

With love and gratitude,
Fabi, Stel & big brother Thomas

We receive hundreds of e-mails and messages of support. Everyone in our lives knew about the voyage of infertility and they were happy to know that we had one new addition to our family.

I started to accept what was, without wanting to manipulate or change it.

From that moment on, I fully embraced the following words that my friend Christian wrote to me. "From this day onward, you can begin at once to live and count each separate day as a new and separate life. Life is always right."

I had a conscious choice to make. I was observing my life and saw that ahead of me were two paths. Somehow, I felt like Alice, from Lewis Carroll's classic *Alice's Adventures in Wonderland*, except I had the Drink Me bottle in one hand and the mushroom in the other; one potion to make me grow, the other to shrink me. One path would lead to heavy emotions, more trauma, sadness and darkness. The second path would force me to enact and really *live* all the lessons I had learned. This second path would lead to growth, empowerment, and somehow – out of this seemingly tragic event - happiness and a deeper sense of purpose. I had seen people who chose the first path; it is a deep abyss. I chose the second path; I chose the light. It seemed like a difficult choice at first, but instinctively I knew it was the correct path for me. My whole life led me to this opportunity to take 100% responsibility for my life and my happiness.

These events in my life made me think about the idiom in the *eye of the storm*. I don't think I had fully understood that until I started this chapter of my life. I always tried to understand the meaning of English expressions in English - not translating them into Portuguese - because most of them don't make sense when translated.

This one in particular, I had to live to feel its meaning.

I pictured myself in a tropical cyclone or hurricane, my entire world spinning fast, not knowing where or even if we would touch down. I always had that image in my head during this time. Then, I understood the eye part of it. In the centre of the cyclone, where there are no clouds, the wind drops away to give a sense of calm. It doesn't mean the storm is over, things may in fact get worse. My lesson from the analogy was for me to learn to be in the eye - to remain calm - while a storm was happening all around me.

CHAPTER 8
NICU

"There are only two ways to live your life. One is as though nothing is a miracle. The other is as though everything is a miracle."

– *Albert Einstein*

I once read a story about two warring tribes in the Andes. One lived high in the mountains and the other in the lowlands. The mountain people invaded the low land, kidnapping a baby with the intent of raising it in the mountains as one of their own.

The people from of the lowlands did not know how to climb the mountain to save the baby. They didn't know the trails that would lead to the settlement nor how to track the kidnappers up the steep mountain. Regardless, they decided to send their strongest fighting men to rescue the baby. The men tried different methods of climbing and they tried to advance up the mountain by many different trails. After endless days, they had conquered only a few hundred feet. They came to the conclusion that unless you were born on the mountain, you could not climb it. The men felt hopeless and prepared to return home.

As they were turning to leave, they saw the baby's mother walking toward them. To their astonishment, the mother was climbing down the mountain that they had not been able to conquer. And she wasn't alone, she was carrying the baby strapped to her back. One man asked how she had climbed a seemingly impassable mountain and rescued her child. She shrugged her shoulders and said, "It wasn't your baby."

My life had changed and I had to adapt very quickly. I had to figure out how to climb that mountain. My feelings of grief were overshadowed by the responsibilities of being a NICU mom. The pain was with me every day, every hour and minute for the coming weeks. I sometimes felt like a caterpillar, inside a cocoon, where it is dark and isolated. Yet, I had made my conscious choice and knew that inevitably I would break free.

The few hours that I spent at home were very difficult. I would become stiff and stop breathing each time the phone rang. The fear of more bad news was constant. I wanted to be at the hospital, with Gabriel, all the time. The vow to myself made me get out of bed to hug Thomas and enjoy my time with him.

Going back to the hospital for the first time was a trip I wish I could forget. Being physically weak, it was difficult to move and every bump on the road jarred my body, causing the C-section incision to scream out to me. The physical pain paled in comparison to the emotional trauma I felt during these first few days. Slowly, I made my way down the long corridors of the hospital, arriving exhausted, to the NICU on the 7th floor.

The nurse said that I could hold Gabriel for the first time. I had to remove all jewelry, as well as my shirt and bra, replacing it with a hospital gown opening to the front. I sat down on a chair close to the incubator while Stel observed the complexity of bringing him out. The nurse picked up Gabriel, still connected to so many machines, and placed him on my chest. I smiled as he squirmed and snuggled on my chest, as if he was searching for my heartbeat. His little body felt very warm. I was elated to finally hold my baby, but apprehensive. He was so tiny that I wasn't even sure how to hold him. He was the size of a Barbie doll: long, skinny, and narrow. I remember holding my breath, fearing that any movement I made would disconnect one of the machines, monitors or wires that he was connected to, that were keeping him alive. It was euphoric to hold him and marvel at his strength.

As the days passed, going to the hospital had become my work. My life was a stream of trips to and from the hospital. Stel would drop Thomas off at day care and since my parents were in Toronto, my father would drive me to Mount Sinai each morning. Every day I seemed to add another hour to my visit.

On the twelfth day, it was my 40th birthday. Before my world collapsed, I had been wanting to host a party and celebrate the beginning of a new decade in my life. Upon hearing of Michael's malformed heart and his prognosis, my desire to celebrate had ceased. On the morning of my birthday, Stel and Thomas prepared a special breakfast at home. They presented me with cake and balloons, with the hope of bringing some joy into our home. In the middle of the celebration, the phone rang: unknown number. That was how calls from Mount Sinai appeared. The familiar feeling of falling out of control, crept over me. The nurse was calling to tell me that Gabriel had very laboured breathing on the CPAP machine and he had to be intubated. I hadn't the slightest idea what that meant, if it was serious or what the complications could be. She sensed my confusion and concisely explained that intubated means placing a flexible plastic tube into the trachea (windpipe) to maintain an open airway.

The nurse who was working that day was named Karen. She explained to me in greater detail why intubation was necessary and that it is very common in micro-preemie babies. With babies so young, their lungs had not fully developed, making breathing on their own extremely difficult. Essentially it was too much effort for Gabriel's lungs. I did have one thing to celebrate that day though, he had reached the one-kilogram milestone. I was elated by that. I felt emotionally fragile during the first few days, asking Stel to call the unit for updates before I went in and again before I went to sleep each night. I had become terrified of more bad news. At least if I heard it at home, from Stel, I felt I would be better able to cope.

One of the most difficult things during this time was that my little Gabriel was not in the same house as me, in a room next to mine where I could give him a good night kiss. Instead, he was kilometers from me and those who loved him, in an incubator with only strangers around him.

Stel was with me one morning when a young doctor came to introduce himself. He said that his name was Dr. Dan and that he wanted to give us an update on Gabriel. I walked away. How much can one person take? Dr. Dan chased me down the unit and tried to talk to me. I told him that I didn't want to know at that moment; that Stel would tell me later. This strategy was so that Stel could translate the doctor language in a manner I could understand, as well as saving me from the *what could happen* portion.

Dr. Dan convinced me that as Gabriel's mom, I had the right and responsibility of knowing. I decided to give it a try. He took a piece of paper and as a kindergarten teacher would do, he drew a heart and patiently explained to me. He said that a PDA, patent ductus arteriosus, was a congenital heart defect where a part of the heart – the ductus arteriosus – fails to close after birth, a common condition in premature babies. This was what a previous doctor had tried to explain to me, but I had shut down at the time. This time I was ready and willing to hear the information and learn. He explained that with medication, it sometimes closes. In Gabriel's case, after one round of the medication, it closed. There was no need for surgical intervention. I sighed with relief.

The conversation with Dr. Dan had a profound impact on me. The nurse working with Gabriel that day was a kind woman named Edna. I told her about the conversation and the change in my perspective about learning and knowing about my son's conditions and health. She told me that for interested parents, Mount Sinai had information classes every Tuesday evening. She suggested that I attend, and I did.

It was my third week at the hospital when I decided to attend the education session the hospital offered. It was in the classroom, a few doors down from the NICU. I was a little nervous, not knowing what to expect. The chairs were placed in a circle where some dads, but predominantly moms, sat. Most of the moms seemed to know each other quite well, chatting in a familiar manner. One mom looked polished, with perfect hair and makeup. In contrast, I was still in maternity clothes and couldn't walk upright. I hadn't looked at my blow dryer and styling products, never mind open my makeup drawer in what seemed like an eternity. All of that, so important to me before, was completely irrelevant. Still, that mom looked great – I don't know how.

A doctor walked in, introducing herself and then each of the parents was asked to do the same. We stated our names and the details about our child in the NICU. I was surprised to learn that some families had been a part of the NICU family for three or four months; clearly I had a lot to learn. I did not ask any questions that first evening, I just listened and absorbed.

Day after day, I was spending even longer hours at Gabriel's bedside. Instead of getting ready for work as most people do, I got ready for the hospital each morning. Rather than a purse and lunch bag, I carried a backpack containing a breast pump and containers to store my milk. I kept daily logs to know how much I had pumped and my freezer at home was full of pink-lid containers – similar to the ones used for urine samples. Each label had Gabriel's name and the time and date that the milk was pumped. I always included a little heart, so he knew how much he was loved.

Pumping was hard work, but I did it with a tenderness of heart, knowing it would be nourishing my child. I would sit in a small white room with florescent lighting and nothing else, pumping for twenty minutes at a time, every three hours. The lactation consultant from the NICU made me aware of the positive impact that mother's milk can make to a baby, especially one as young and fragile as Gabriel. My nipples were sore and chapped, but Gabriel was my priority. I was producing so much milk that my freezer at home was full and I ended up donating the excess to the breast milk donor bank where it would be used for a study.

Edna started to teach me how to care for Gabriel. She showed me how to change his diaper without pulling any wires loose, how to take his temperature, how to clean his soulful eyes, now that they were open. I wondered if he could see the outline of his mama although I knew he could feel my love. I realized that all the baby books were written from the perspective of a full-term pregnancy. There was nothing about how to care for a premature child that should still be developing in its mother's womb. Edna told me that on days when he wasn't stable enough to be removed from the incubator, I could hold his finger and how I should touch his delicate skin. She encouraged me to talk to him and read him stories.

Karen taught me about the ventilator and how to monitor the levels of CO_2 (carbon dioxide) in Gabriel's blood. She explained with the patience of a saint, the meaning of all the different machines and alarms and most importantly, how to read his monitor. I watched him struggling to take each breath but looking into his eyes, I saw a tenacious will to live. He was teaching me the power of perseverance and how to overcome anything that presented it-self as adversity. My little baby was teaching me, just by being who he was. He seemed so fragile, yet he was a fierce little fighter.

Slowly, I found my place in the NICU. Slowly, I started to feel like Gabriel's mom. This was a magnificent accomplishment for me. When I arrived there, I didn't have a place. The doctors, nurses, therapists, fellows and residents all went to Gabriel's bedside to check him, but I didn't know what to do.

As most new parents, I took for granted the fact that I brought Thomas home three days after his birth. He was a big baby, 4 ki-los 195 grams (9 pounds, 4 ounces). We had prepared a beautiful room for him - a quiet space with classical music at times. There was a round area rug with elephants on its perimeter and a soft night light so I could watch him while he slept. I was the one who made the decisions about when to bathe him, feed him, change him and when we would go out.

Having a baby living at the hospital was such a different expe-rience. I could not make any decisions in the beginning. I was a spectator in my child's life. I sat for hours, watching him struggle for each breath, watching him being fed through a feeding tube, seeing medicine enter by a PICC line.

I wondered if he was in pain. He couldn't cry because of the breathing tube in his nose and the feeding tube in his mouth.

It didn't take me long to understand the importance of a work-

---

A PICC line is a peripherally inserted central catheter. It is used if a baby is expected to need an IV for an extended period of time to deliver medication. Source: *www.aboutkidshealth.ca*

ing relationship between the bedside nurses and myself. Gabriel's main nurses, Edna and Karen, started to *translate* the NICU for me. I began to see the routine and understand the terminology that was used; it was the language that was used in my new world. I became confident and immersed myself in caring for him. I became the one giving the updates to Stel on what happened to Gabriel during the day before he visited him in the evening.

The hospital was doing a research study on a program called Family Integrated Care, FICare. The purpose was to bring families to the bedside and teach parents how to take a larger role in caring for infants while they remained in the unit. I was invited to participate once Gabriel was free from the ventilator. Being a part of the FICare study allowed me to hold my son skin-to-skin (kangaroo care) most of the time that I was there. It gave me the opportunity to participate in the daily education sessions with different professionals such as dieticians, pharmacists, therapists and neonatologists. I learned about the development of a premature baby and how to encourage them to have tummy time in the hospital and at home.

I had to present my child during the medical rounds, also referred to as multidisciplinary rounds. These are an important part of the patient care process involving doctors, nurses, dieticians, pharmacists and respiratory therapists. This was very intimidating at first, as the average team was eight to nine medical professionals. I eventually gained enough confidence to ask questions and then gained the knowledge to know *what* to ask. After a time, the doctors started asking me questions about Gabriel because I was there for so many hours each day. It was an incredible partnership. I was finally involved in every aspect of Gabriel's life, even making decisions *with* the medical team. Being a part of that program empowered me as a mother and I learned what it means to advocate for your child.

I was understanding the lessons of that unwelcome journey. I started to believe that anything was possible. I saw determination and perseverance coming from my preterm baby. He inspired me to continue to believe in meeting my goals, as that is what that tiny human did every day in the NICU. He also taught me to be tolerant and have more patience. Perhaps he was the best teacher I have had so far in my life.

CHAPTER 9
Finding the Joy

"I saw the angel in the marble and carved until I set him free."
— *Michelangelo*

I was sitting in a circle at a workshop. One of the facilitators was softly playing a drum while he began reciting the words of Constantine P. Cavafy's magnificent poem *Ithaka*. Each word touched my heart and my soul. I devoured how he spoke of the journey of life. *Ithaka* is based on Homer's story of Odysseus' journey home. It speaks about life in all its complexities, describing both the setbacks and the positive memories. It uses adventures to symbolize the challenges and the experiences which will make us stronger. It's not about the destination; it's about the journey, the learning along the way. The last two verses came to me, while I was in the NICU, telling me how to survive this part of my journey:

Have Ithaka always in your mind.
Your arrival there is what you are destined for.
But don't in the least hurry the journey.
Better it last for years,
so that when you reach the island you are old,
rich with all you have gained on the way,

not expecting Ithaka to give you wealth.
Ithaka gave you a splendid journey.
Without her you would not have set out.
She hasn't anything else to give you.

And if you find her poor, Ithaka hasn't deceived you.
So wise you have become, of such experience,
that already you'll have understood what these Ithakas mean.

Hours were turning into days, days turning to weeks and weeks into months. I had no control over my circumstances, but I could choose how I responded to them. I could use the power of my mind to find a different perspective on the events I was living.

I had spent years working on the evolution of my being. Stel and I had worked with the top trainers in the world, learning to unlock the powers of the mind. I had coached dozens of women and read what seemed like libraries full of books on self-development and growth. I had a strong sense of who I was; I had gotten to know myself well. I had experienced peace within and deep fulfillment. Rather than thinking of my time at the NICU as something I had to endure, I started recognizing that it was an opportunity to put in practice all the theories and lessons I had learned. I was choosing to make this a positive experience, rather than a chance to wallow in self-pity and sadness.

Walking into the NICU the first time was like walking into the unknown. Everything changed in a split second. It was a change, but not necessarily a negative one. I heard over and over that in the NICU, it was one step forward and two back. Every day before I walked in I would ground myself and then I would visualize Michael floating on top of his brother's incubator. In my heart, he was there, protecting his brother, helping him to take that one step forward each day.

My day at the hospital began in the early morning, asking for an update from the nurse. I would check Gabriel's chart to see how much weight he gained overnight. Some days it was ten grams and others it was thirty. I celebrated each gram. Edna taught me something new each day. She taught me how to parent and love my baby through the glass. She taught me to see past the tubes and machines, to the child that needed me; she showed me that I had to celebrate my son. His alarms were always being set off, mostly the one for his oxygen levels as they fluctuated so frequently. Some mornings Edna looked apprehensive; I never dared to ask why. Those days I celebrated that Gabriel had lived one more day.

Many days when I arrived in the NICU, I noticed that some of the babies were no longer there. I knew that some were transferred to other hospitals. The others I did not ask about. The nurses never told me. There was a silence between us that said the child had passed. Once I saw a team rushing to a bedside close to mine, placing a screen around them for privacy, but it was so thin that I saw everything. The mother held her child while the respiratory therapist was adjusting the breathing equipment. She held her baby until his last breath. A solemnness fell over the NICU that day and each day a soul left the unit. Death happens at hospitals, however, in the NICU, the nurses care for their patients so closely and with such love that each time, a loss is felt.

The mother and baby were hastily whisked out of the ward. When the screen was removed, I looked at the floor and saw a mess of breathing tubes, sterile packaging ripped open and discarded, tape and whatever else that was used to try to save the baby's life. I met the eyes of a friend I had made in the unit. Voula and I could see the heavy heart in each other and the pain we felt for the mother that we did not know, who had just held her child as he passed away.

Looking at my own son, knowing it could have been him, I felt blessed. He had so many bad days, so many infections and so many days when doctors told me he was very sick. I chose to, at those times especially, focus on the positive. If I was told that he had 15% chance of developing a certain condition, I would immediately reframe that and hear that he had an 85% chance of staying healthy. I looked for the good.

I recalled hearing my friend relay an analogy from Zig Ziglar's book See You at the Top. It was something to the effect that when you're mining for gold, you had to move tons of dirt. But you had to keep in mind that you were not interested in the dirt, you were only looking for the gold. Every day in the NICU I looked for the gold. Sometimes there was but a speck, and I rejoiced in that speck. This, among other things I had learned along the way, allowed me to fully accept the journey I was a part of. This positive mental attitude transformed the way I experienced the NICU, surrendering to the situation and embracing it, rather than resisting. Gabriel's bed was on a very busy corner of the NICU. I called it Yonge-Dundas Square – the busiest intersection in Toronto. A place similar to Times Square in New York. The unit was always lit with the industrial strength fluorescent lights, without windows allowing any natural light to stream in. I never had any concept of the weather outside, no glimpse of the sun or sky. Only the large, hospital-style clock on the wall above Gabriel's bed kept me aware of time.

During the day, there was a lot of traffic at my Yonge-Dundas square. There were doctors, residents, desk clerks, therapists and nurses coming and going in a regular stream throughout the day. When the new babies arrived, they passed through our corner. I watched the mothers who had just delivered their preemies walking in for the first time, that familiar ghostly look on their face.

From my chair, beside bed 25, I could see most of the other incubators and would often chat with the other mothers. We watched each other's babies, creating an informal support group within the unit. I became particularly good friends with two other mothers named Voula and Kerri. They were my NICU buddies, we gave each other strength, celebrating the accomplishments of our babies together. We cried for each other's babies, we cried when a baby passed away. We said goodbye to many families that were ready to take their child home for the first time. I longed for the day that I could take my baby home as well, making my daily visualization as I left the hospital, a reality.

Gabriel's nurse Karen told me that babies are usually discharged around their due date. My due date was August 22nd. I created a vision board at home where I wrote the date, Gabriel's daily accomplishments, his weight and a countdown to August 22nd. This made coming home every evening enjoyable, and it broke down the journey into manageable steps. Each evening I would think that we were one day closer to Gabriel living in his rightful home.

Each evening as I drove down College Street – a cosmopolitan street filled with restaurants, bars and patios – I saw so much life. While I rushed home after a day in the NICU, I saw people enjoying the hot summer months by riding their bikes and eating on patios with their families and friends. I too longed to take a walk outside, feel the warmth of the sun in the day and enjoy the hot summer nights; in reality, I was too exhausted to do any of that.

When I arrived at home each evening, I was there just in time to have dinner with Stel and catch up with what was important before he left for the hospital. Our conversations were brief. He took over all my daily responsibilities, such as banking and grocery shopping, so I could focus on Gabriel and spending some quality time with Thomas. Sometimes, we left him at his cousin's house so we could have a quick dinner date near the hospital. We knew we had to nurture our marriage. We cared immensely for each other and we wanted each other to feel supported. On our wedding anniversary, Stel surprised me and made all the arrangements for us to have a nice dinner, watch a movie at the Toronto International Film Festival and spend the night in a hotel. For one night, I felt everything could go back to normal.

Every night, I watched some cartoons with Thomas before bed. I loved snuggling with him on the sofa during this time. He gave me a reason to smile each evening, a reason to carry on after the end-less hours in the vinyl hospital chair. I tucked him in each night, reading him his favourite books and watching him fall asleep. I watched how easily and effortlessly he breathed. I was grateful for him each night. I thought about my time away from him; the things we weren't doing together at this time. I thought about all the fun we had together prior to the pregnancy, all of this seemed like a distant memory. That time was gone. Luckily, a good friend of mine reminded me that he was only three years old and this time away from him was only temporary and short, considering that I had a whole life with him. Again, this shift in perspective allowed me to further enjoy my journey and add more positive emotions to my being.

Every day, as I walked through the hospital corridors or took the elevator, I looked at each person's eyes and wondered about their own stories; what was happening in their lives. Patients, staff and visitors all have particular expressions. I looked at each one, trying to guess what they were experiencing. There was sadness, worry, joy. Feelings that we have in real life but they seem to be magnified in a hospital setting.

A man may have had just become a father, another person might just have received news of an unexpected diagnosis, others may have been waiting patiently for the recovery of a loved one, perhaps some were visiting a relative for the last time. Others had puzzled faces, maybe because they did not comprehend the medical explanation of their condition. I saw many immigrants who perhaps didn't speak English and were facing those situations a long way from the familiarity of their homeland.

I felt compassion for each person. As I had learned to look past the equipment to see and celebrate Gabriel, I looked past people's outer appearances and reactions to the daily events going straight to their hearts, their essence. This was a beautiful place to be: learning not to judge, but to evaluate.

Being in the NICU was very isolating. Or perhaps I isolated myself. I couldn't call my friends just to tell them that Gabriel had ten spells in one day or that he was feeding 40ml of milk at a time. I was too exhausted to explain things to them and I didn't want to hear about anything that I would consider trivial at the moment, considering I was dealing with life and death, each day at the hospital. I made a choice to go inward; it helped me to focus. Very few people came to visit in the hospital and they were always short visits, thankfully. I was too tired to be a good hostess in the NICU and didn't want to take time away from Gabriel to be social. I knew, though, that we had a tremendous number of people cheering for him, sending him love and positive vibes. That was enough for me at that time.

My daily routine consisted of at least two hours of driving to and from the hospital, hours of breast pumping and writing a journal for Gabriel. The balance of my twelve-hour day was sitting at his bedside. I used some of this time to reflect about the turns my life had taken. I did not think ahead to what my life would look like after, with the exception of the daily visualization of leaving the hospital as a family.

I tried to have most of my focus totally immersed on the present, in the NICU, in a positive manner. I would not allow my mind to complain. I could not change or remove myself from the situation, so there was no point in dwelling on it. Embracing it made me feel empowered, that I was at cause and not at effect to the situation. Any negative thought that came in my mind was released, without judgement. I had learned that thoughts are powerful and create tangible results in our lives. Our thoughts lead our feelings. I felt pain when I was trying to resist what was occurring, but the second I stayed in the present, the suffering disappeared; I felt love on so many levels. I was feeling unconditional love for my little son as well as the love for the nurses who wholeheartedly cared for the tiny souls and their families.

The days were long but I was comfortable in my new environment. I enjoyed speaking with all the members of the NICU team. I got to know the nurses, fellows and the front desk ladies who always greeted me with smiles and hugs. It felt like a second family, in that fluorescent-lit medical room. The front desk ladies, Gloria and Elaine treated me as if I was their own daughter, always wishing me a good day and reminding me to take some time to care for myself. I remember Maureen, a social worker, who always seemed to know when something wasn't right. I ended up calling her My Little Witch, for her sixth sense.

Another member of my hospital family was Marianne, a parent-resource nurse. She taught most of the education classes that I attended at the hospital. Marianne had a profound compassion that could be heard in her voice and genuine care for others. In a way, she reminded me of my mom. She taught me the benefits of touch, the healing power of holding my tiny child, not only for him, but for me. It was Marianne that told me that I had to take a mandatory CPR (cardiopulmonary resuscitation) course before discharge. Never in my mind did I conceive that the short course would prove to save the life of my baby, shortly after his discharge. Karen and I spent hours chatting. We talked about life, careers, children, marriage, food, travel. She was not only Gabriel's nurse, she became my friend. Our friendship grew as she adjusted my son's oxygen levels, completed blood tests, and weighed diapers. Yes, we had to weigh the diapers to compare the input and output, and each time we laughed. She had a magical manner about her, an ability to take my mind away from the darker side of the NICU, if it happened to meander there for a moment, without me catching it. Her magic made the day seem normal, even when my baby was having a trying day.

Edna, or Mama Bear as I lovingly referred to her, was a pillar of strength in the NICU. When Gabriel was a bit older and stronger, she loved to dress him and cut the tape that held this oxygen tubes in place into little hearts. She showed me how to bathe such a tiny baby and how to carefully weigh him. She spent countless hours teaching me how to care for him. She was my main teacher when I was preparing for family meetings with the medical team. Each day she prepared me to present updates about Gabriel to the multi-disciplinary medical team, during their daily rounds.

One day a doctor told me that he was going to try to extubate Gabriel, freeing him from mechanical ventilation, that afternoon. I was very apprehensive. My gut instinct or mother's instinct, or both, told me it wasn't the correct time to do so. Extubation had been attempted the week before and it failed. He had been on a ventilator for over six weeks and needed to come off soon. I didn't feel that Gabriel was stable enough that day, but the doctor insisted.

I stepped outside and waited impatiently. When I went back in, I saw Gabriel's face without any tubes. He had the face of an angel, so beautiful, so perfect. My heart stopped, my eyes welled up, truly seeing my miracle child for the first time after six weeks. The respiratory therapist told me I could kiss him. I will feel that kiss, his tender face, on my lips forever. The CPAP machine, which covered most of his face again, was replaced. I was watching his oxygen levels drop further and further. Finally, I was asked to leave. An hour passed. I sat alone in the NICU waiting area, trying to stay positive and present, but my instinct told me it was not going well.

Finally, the doctor who recommended the extubation, exited the unit and was walking toward me. He hugged me and then motioned for us to walk. He apologized, saying that he felt stupid, not waiting for results from a blood test that had been done that morning. The blood test revealed that Gabriel had an infection and that if he had known he wouldn't have tried the extubation. Gabriel was back on a ventilator and had started a round of antibiotics. Perhaps I should have been angry, but I wasn't. I was concerned about Gabriel's infection, but I had an inner voice telling me he would be alright. Somehow, this experience showed me the human side of the doctors in the unit. I was moved by his honesty. This was one of the most memorable days in the NICU as I realized that everything in life was an illusion; everything was what I chose to perceive it as. I'm the one who gave meaning to each situation. Essentially, it was what my teachers had been telling me for years: that there were no inherently *bad* or *good* events, just events. How I chose to interpret them was up to me.

One week later, after the infection had cleared, Gabriel was given steroids and the extubation was attempted again. There was a time frame in which this medication could help babies most effectively and his window was closing. After three days of that medication Gabriel was successfully extubated. He was breathing with only the support of the CPAP machine. It was a monumental step for him. I felt a milestone had been reached.

I was celebrating internally, but the tenuous nature of the NICU, always made me feel cautious.

A gift from our tour guide in Tikal, Benedicto, was a book called *The Book of Destiny* by Carlos Barrios. The words in the book explained that the past did not exist, it existed. It stated that the present is only a memory and the future did not yet exist. The book stated "There is only this instant, this very moment, the eternal present." This was to become my mantra in the NICU.

When I was present, truly present, I saw Gabriel as a miracle.

It was a wonder, in the purest sense of the word, to see a 900-gram baby reach one kilo, then double his weight to two kilograms and so forth. It was a phenomenon to see this baby open his eyes for the first time. I watched in pure awe as his purple skin peeled away, transforming into the familiar and healthy-looking, pinkish baby skin and cartilage form the shape of his ears. All of this development occurs inside the womb, during the last of the forty weeks of gestation. I was witnessing the miracle and wonder of the creation of a human body.

When I was truly present, I was able to watch in happiness and in gratitude, all of the technology that exists to keep these tiny beings alive. I was able to feel and appreciate the love that is given to the babies by everyone at Mount Sinai, from the delivery room to the NICU.

In that place of being present, I felt an overwhelming love. Love that I did not know existed. The medical teams and especially the nurses cared for the babies as their own. I had a preconceived idea that after so many years in such an emotionally intense profession, one would become immune. Yet, I saw hearts at work, day after day. Mama Bear's eyes would shine with pure elation for every one of Gabriel's accomplishments, like the day he moved from an incubator to a crib. It was with her that I dressed my baby for the first time in a beautiful white outfit. We were a part of the NICU for so long that it truly was my second home, some days I would spend more hours in that unit than in my actual house.

It was easy for me to stay positive and present because I was surrounded by love. Having the support of the nurses while in the NICU made all the difference in my life at that time. My gratitude to them is eternal.

On Gabriel's due date, August 22nd, I had expected to be packing up and heading home with him, fulfilling my daily visualization as I exited on Murray Street.

As the date approached, I recognized that he was far from being ready to be discharged. He had developed Retinopathy of Prematurity (ROP), one of the top causes of blindness in infancy.

This condition caused him to have to be temporarily transferred to Sick Kids, just across the street from Mount Sinai Hospital for a procedure.

All the hospitals in the immediate area are connected via underground tunnels, so a transport team came to transfer him through the tunnels. The nurses and other mothers all cried and hugged me. Their eyes told me that I could find the strength to go on, to be strong for my little miracle baby.

I carried the strength I had found and the lessons I had learned in the NICU with me. It is only through the other people in that unit, all of them, that I mustered the strength to face the daily challenges. I even found enough strength inside of me to comfort and support the newly arriving parents in the ward. Somehow, the newbies looked up to the parents who had been there longer. I suppose it was to learn how we were all holding it together. I know

---

Retinopathy of Prematurity is a disease of premature babies that causes abnormal blood vessels to grow in the retina, the layer of nerve tissue in the eye that enables us to see. This growth can cause the retina to detach from the back of the eye, leading to blindness. *Source: www.kidshealth.org*

that I gave them hope and the belief that they could do it as well.

For many years I had believed that I was living in the present moment, while making plans for the future and setting goals. Perhaps I was living in the present to my ability at that particular point in time. Only now did I have a full realization of *what living in the present* actually meant. Prior to this experience, my mind was always ahead of me. I was always thinking of the future. Even when I was playing with Thomas, I would be thinking about what we could do when he was eight or ten years of age. I was always planning our next trip, the next course I would enroll in, the next book I would read or the next project I wanted to complete. If I wasn't doing that, I was mentally compiling a list of things I wanted to accomplish the next day or the items to be added to my weekly grocery list.

I truly believe in the power of goal-setting and this will never change. The magic happens when we set goals for the future, accepting and honouring the present moment, fully in a state of gratitude because the purpose of the goal is to provide a journey. The NICU taught me the real meaning of staying present. The present moment is all we have. It allowed me to move away from any residual fears that I had. I had learned the lesson before, but now it was ingrained in me. We only feel fear because we anticipate what *could* happen, like having a bear encounter. However, when we stay present, really present, and focus on what is actually happening, fear dissipates and is replaced by a deep, resounding and pure love.

In this place of love, my faith in humanity was restored. Those that I would have once called strangers were a family to me. The *strangers* went far beyond my expectations to save the life of my child. This new family supported my family on so many levels. I saw the gold in every human being. I saw the love that we all have inside that tends to be masked by our daily lives and what I now know to be irrelevant problems. I now saw that behind each mask was a human being, a being of love, with a story. I could imagine a world where all people saw this in themselves and each other, where all people would look for the gold, rather than judge based on differences in behaviour, affluence or skin colour.

Learning how to truly live in the now allowed me to see love, feel love and celebrate the smallest things. I didn't know at the time that it was the beginning of my healing process and the full acceptance of my life. I didn't know that this journey would lead me down another, even more fulfilling path.

Born out of this *tragedy* was my real purpose in life. I learned to speak about infertility, the NICU experience, the loss of Michael and the outcomes of premature birth without feeling pain. This ability would really and truly help others who had great needs, which is all I ever wanted to do.

CHAPTER 10
Living in Gratitude

"Gratitude unlocks the fullness of life. It turns what we have into enough, and more. It turns denial into acceptance, chaos to order, confusion to clarity. It can turn a meal into a feast, a house into a home, a stranger into a friend. Gratitude makes sense of our past, brings peace for today and creates a vision for tomorrow."

– Melody Beattie

Growing up in Brazil, I was always very thankful for the things I had because around every corner, I would see someone struggling to live. As a result, I grew up with a great appreciation for my life. I always felt very fortunate to have supportive parents who allowed me to do the things I always dreamed of doing. They allowed me to choose my own career, they allowed me to set foot outside Brazil and supported me in all my travels. They stood behind me when I decided to move to Canada to get married, even though I was going to live and build a family far away from them. I always had big dreams. Things always turned out to have the outcome I wished or planned for. Being grateful came naturally to me, it was a part of me.

The NICU tested me in many ways, including my core values, gratitude being one of them. After the first weeks in the NICU, when it became my home away from home, when the world didn't seem as foggy anymore, when the reality had sunk in, I started to feel a very powerful emotion inside me. It took me a while to realize that my heart was immersed in gratitude. Some may think that it was a strange thing to feel gratitude in such a clinical and often sad place. It was my choice to see the good in the NICU, it was my choice to see things to be grateful for, and that was what I focused on. That feeling stayed with me and grew, allowing me to do more than just survive the months I was at the hospital.

The first while it was impossible to feel gratitude for what was happening. I was feeling so much pain, I was in denial and I was beyond feeling overwhelmed. Once I started to focus on the good, I was then able to embrace the situation and accept it. I had to, however, constantly monitor my thoughts. I welcomed the negative thoughts as they showed up, trying to understand where they came from. Then, I worked hard to dismiss them. Days when I talked to other families and learned what was happening with their babies, I wondered if it could happen to mine too. Then, I immediately changed my fear into hope, and reminded myself that every baby is different and just because one baby developed a certain condition, didn't mean mine would too. Sometimes I even felt exhausted by the process of changing my thoughts. Some days, it was very hard to stay focused on the good when Gabriel's condition was unstable for so long.

One day, when I arrived at the hospital, I was told that Gabriel had been moved to the level two nursery. Every parent wanted their child to go to level two, because it meant that their baby was no longer in critical condition and could breathe with less support. I was surprised. I didn't think he was stable enough to be transferred yet. Nonetheless, I became excited as I felt that it was one step closer to going home.

As soon as I went into the nursery, I saw on Edna's face that she wasn't comfortable with Gabriel being there. She looked worried because his oxygen level kept dropping. He had been on low-flow oxygen for two days prior to this transfer, a much milder way to provide breathing support than the CPAP machine. Both Edna and I knew he was tired of breathing on his own. We called the doctor because he didn't look well.

Immediately, the doctor transferred him back to the level three NICU where we had been for so many months. Then, the doctor on-call suspected he had an infection and had to do a lumbar puncture I became angry, very angry. I couldn't believe he had to go through such a potentially risky and painful procedure. I cried for him.

I didn't want my baby to feel pain. I believed he had been transferred prematurely and he was just tired and needed to go back on the CPAP machine. Later on that day, the result of the test came back negative. He did not have an infection and I breathed in relief. This is why so many people call the NICU an emotional roller coaster; you must learn to live day-by-day and sometimes hour-by-hour as everything can change so fast.

Constantly monitoring my thoughts was very hard work because of the nature of the NICU. Nevertheless, I had a deep knowingness that all that transpired was changing my life and making me a stronger and better person. I knew that however difficult the

---

A lumbar puncture is a test during which a special, thin needle is inserted into the space that surrounds the spinal cord in the lower back to collect a sample of CSF, cerebral spinal fluid. Usually done to rule out infection. *Source: www.sickkids.ca*

journey was, it would have a very positive outcome.

People often ask me today how I could be grateful for being in that situation. My answer is: How could I not be? I was grateful to be at Mount Sinai Hospital because they acted very fast when things turned bad. I was grateful to every single person involved in Gabriel's care. I was grateful that every day I had him for one more day, I was grateful that I was a mom, after struggling with infertility. I was grateful that Gabriel had a personal angel watching over him.

From spring to summer and summer to fall. The seasons were changing. I was trying to manage life at home. Thomas had just started Montessori school, which was a big transition for him. He had to adjust to a new school, new friends and a new teacher. I was gone for so long and my three-year-old was growing fast. I had missed the entire summer of fun. I had missed his first roller coaster ride. Throughout this time, I kept reminding myself that we had the rest of our lives together, that this was a temporary situation.

Every Sunday we brought Thomas to the hospital. Part of the FICare program was to bring families together. I was grateful that the hospital allowed siblings inside the unit. One of our respiratory therapists, Karla, taught Thomas how to dance. She was always prepared to give him colouring sheets and crayons to decorate his baby brother's incubator. Stel made the visits fun for Thomas, always making it an adventure. They even became best friends with the owner of a hot dog stand across the street from Mount Sinai.

He seemed to be coping well with all the changes in his life and Stel and I made sure he felt how much we love him.

The leaves started to change colour and the drive to the hospital became more scenic. Some days I took the subway but preferred to drive. I needed to see the sunlight and feel the air blowing on my face after so many hours of sitting in a room without a window. It was at the end of September when Gabriel was transferred to the level two nursery again. This time he was ready. Most of the babies are transferred to another hospital, usually to a location that is closer to home. Gabriel stayed at Sinai, as I had wished, but only because he developed ROP and had to go for a procedure and follow-ups at Sick Kids. He had to have his eyes checked on a weekly basis for the first two months, then monthly. After the first year, the checks were every six months and remain as such to this day.

The first week he was in the level two nursery, we had a family meeting. It was an exciting day for me, as I knew we would be setting goals and preparing to go home. There were quite a few people in that meeting: Dr. Yenge, the in-service neonatologist, our nurse, the social worker, the discharge nurse, my husband and myself. The doctor was very straightforward when she broke the news that when Gabriel was discharged he would require home oxygen. I did not expect that. After all these months I did not want to bring the hospital home with us. I wanted to carry on with life where I had left six months before. "I want to have a normal life," I told her. With a very soft and calm voice, she looked into my eyes and said to me with a lot of compassion, "This will be your new normal." I did not know then the impact that these words would have in my life to this day.

A couple of weeks later, we started the countdown to bring him home. Gabriel had to be on full oral feeds and tolerating every one of them before being discharged. He also had to maintain his oxygen levels without dropping (without having any spells) and he had to pass his car seat test. In the meantime, I had to learn how to handle the oxygen tanks, the portable oxygen monitor and how to prepare his medication.

The days were intense, I spent 14 to 16 hours a day at the hospital trying to breastfeed him so that his feeding tube could be permanently removed. I was exhausted but feeling incredibly accomplished. The determination and endurance that my baby exhibited was beyond inspiring. The expectations of the NICU were high and he was working to achieve them all. And he did! He amazed the entire team. He beat the odds. He was now ready to see the outside world for the first time. He was ready to come to his loving home.

While holding Gabriel at the hospital, I read him books. I described in detail, the world outside, with its beautiful colors and sounds. I told him all the fun things we were going to do. I wanted him to know that it was worth living and that we loved him unconditionally. Thomas talked to him about his adventures at the zoo and the Science Centre and all the things they were going to do together.

Two days before discharge, Stel and I had to sleep at the hospital with Gabriel in a separate room outside the NICU. We had no nurses, no one coming to check on him that night. It was our final preparation.

We had t-shirts printed for the entire family that said Thank You and wore them to the hospital. My parents had come to Toronto to be with us and my in-laws were present as well. Everyone wanted to be a part of bringing Gabriel home. It was the greatest celebration of our lives.

On October 10th, on day 146, my little fighter was ready to go home. I woke up early and put on my blue Thank You t-shirt. The sleeves had pictures of Edna and Karen, our primary nurses, while the front had a big Thank You to the NICU team. I drove to Mount Sinai as I did every morning by myself. Stel would join me later with our parents and Thomas. On the way there, I kept thinking that it was my very last drive with an empty car seat. Next time, I would have my surviving twin, my baby fighter, sitting in it. Walking inside the hospital that day was bitter sweet. I cried in anticipation of how would I say bye to the family I had become a part of and how I would be able to care for Gabriel without their daily support. They reassured me that I was well trained and would be able to take care of Gabriel at home. I knew that, but I also knew I would miss every single person.

I went to Gabriel's bed. That day we had a new nurse, she helped me pack and then I presented Gabriel on the very last medical rounds. The doctor on call that day was Sharon, the doctor Gabriel had on his first day. I was very fond of her. She was so caring that even when she was not working in the unit, she came to see how he was doing.

From 900 grams (two pounds) to over four kilograms (nine pounds), Gabriel had grown so much; he was the pure definition of resilience. He had an incredible will to live. As I said good-bye to every single person that day, I knew I would be back. I knew I had to give back to the hospital that had given us so much.

I put Gabriel in the car seat on the stroller base to take him home, accompanied by his oxygen tank, multiple wires and a monitor. It was quite a logistic feat. When he was ready to go, we took a beautiful picture in front of the unit, with both sets of grandparents and Thomas pushing the stroller. It was the beginning of a new journey; we had just taken the first step.

As we got to the main floor, we walked as a family towards the Murray Street exit. It was the realization of the dream I had visualized for so many months. I was taking Gabriel home in his car seat. He was attached to the oxygen, but my true living miracle was going home.

There were no balloons, no flowers, no teddy bears, no gifts received that day as there had been when Thomas was born and we brought him home. There was a much more significant reward and welcome home gift. We had unconditional love and the accomplishment of surviving a great ordeal.

We found an even greater appreciation for the simple things in life, things that are worth more than anything money could ever buy. I was incredibly grateful to the lessons that experience and my little son had taught me. I truly understood the meaning of acceptance, compassion, understanding, patience and unconditional love. Somewhere I had heard that the true lessons in life took five minutes to learn and a lifetime to master. I thought I had known those things before, but now, I not only knew them, I felt them on a profound level of my being.

My understanding reminded me of the story of Dan Millman, a college professor and a former world-champion athlete. Despite his success, he had a feeling that something was missing from his life. In his book, *Way Of The Peaceful Warrior*, he mentions that life had brought him rewards, but no lasting peace or satisfaction. It wasn't until he met an old man - whom he called Socrates - that became his mentor and friend, did his world change.

Dan realized that he was sleeping prior to their encounter, just dreaming he was awake. "I had always believed that a life of quality, enjoyment and wisdom were my human birthright and would be automatically bestowed upon me as time passed." He goes on to explain that he didn't know that he had to be taught how to live. This parallels the journey I had taken, I had learned the theory of many things, but it wasn't until I was truly tested, did I internalize the lessons.

CHAPTER 11
A New Chapter

"There will come a time when you believe everything is finished.
Yet that will be the beginning."

— Louis L'Amour

It was the beginning of fall. Through the large windows of my family room, I saw the leaves on the trees changing color. It's the most beautiful season to me. São Paulo does not have well-defined seasons, so when I came to Canada and saw the spectacular colors, I was in awe. My garden was preparing to hibernate and so was I. I was well aware of the fact that Gabriel's immune system wasn't prepared to fight common winter illnesses. I decided that no one would come to visit us and we would not go out, other than to doctor or therapy appointments. That was my plan. I became obsessed with hand washing and hand sanitizer. I had to protect Gabriel. Thomas embraced the changes at home and became a very good helper. He developed a very strong bond with his brother. At such an early age, he understood the intensity of having a medically fragile child at home. He never touched the oxygen tanks or the monitor.

The holiday season was fast approaching. I was excited and grateful that we would all be home, together, this Christmas. I planned to prepare a small celebration for the four of us. However, there were other plans made for us. One evening, mid-way through December, Gabriel started to breathe very heavily. I knew him well and I didn't hesitate to take him to his pediatrician who, after doing a chest x-ray, decided to admit him to hospital with pneumonia. It was a hard week but I was positive he would be better in a matter of days and we would still celebrate Christmas at home.

He did not get better. On December 23rd, early in the morning, I was breastfeeding him in a small single room at our community hospital when he went into respiratory distress. I knew the signs. I did not need to look at the monitor to see that his oxygen saturation was very low. He was turning blue. I started to scream; no one came to help us. I immediately heard Marianne's voice whispering in my head. She was the nurse who taught me CPR at Mount Sinai. I heard her saying that when you don't know what to do, start CPR. I put Gabriel on the bed and I started doing CPR. Looking at the monitor, I saw that his saturation was below fifty, his face was almost navy blue.

A button above the bed caught my eye, it said CODE BLUE I had not noticed that button before. I pushed it and a team came to rescue Gabriel. That moment I collapsed on the floor and someone called my husband who was at work. He arrived at the hospital in just a few minutes. I don't think I want to know how fast he drove that day.

Shortly after that incident, my friend Deedee called to see how things were going; I told her what had just happened. We had

Code Blue is generally used to indicate the need of immediate medical attention been friends for a few years. She had her son prematurely, years before me, so she knew the challenges I had faced. She was also one of the first parent partners at Mount Sinai and was involved with the hospital when I had Gabriel. She suggested that I advocate to have him transferred to Sick Kids hospital where there would be more resources to take care of him. He also had a file at Sick Kids and was being seen by a few specialists there.

Once the Code Blue team stabilized Gabriel, I was allowed back into the room. He was very lethargic and pale, his eyes didn't even blink. He had a blank look on his face. The nurses reassured us that Gabriel was fine, just exhausted from what had happened. I lost my mind because I knew my child best and realized that the local hospital wasn't equipped to take care of a child with higher needs.

I had spent over one thousand hours at his bedside and I was well-trained to recognize Gabriel's needs. Being part of FICare made me a strong advocate for my son; that afternoon everything came full circle. I used all that I had to get him transferred to Sick Kids, where he would receive appropriate care.

I called every doctor I knew from Mount Sinai to help us to have him transferred. It wasn't an easy afternoon. For the first time, I saw Stel become angry with someone. He yelled at the doctor to transfer Gabriel, to save his life as we had already lost one child.

Eventually I was able to speak with of one of the doctors at Mount Sinai, Dr. David, who had given us incredible support since the time I was pregnant. He is one of the most caring human beings I ever met. He guided us on the procedure to follow to have our son transferred.

Many hours later, the doctor in the local hospital agreed to make the transfer, only after reviewing the results of numerous tests done on Gabriel. She finally agreed that he needed more specialized care. When the transport team from Sick Kids arrived, I was relieved. I was in the ambulance with my baby and knew how serious the situation was. He was taken into the emergency department around midnight and soon transferred to the 7th floor. Once he was stable, I went home to rest and spend some time with Thomas.

That day had been so stressful that my milk supply disappeared. I attempted to pump but not one drop of milk came out. I was desperate, my baby needed milk, I kept pumping until I bled.

I tried to get some rest, thinking about the good things that happened that day. It was hard because I was so angry that I had to do CPR on my own son inside a hospital. I fell asleep from total exhaustion.

Early in the morning, I woke up to the phone ringing, it was Stel calling me from the hospital, crying. One more time, I felt my heart stop for a second. Gabriel had coded again and had been transferred to the pediatric intensive care unit (PICU), and was in isolation. I rushed to the hospital. I saw him breathing on CPAP, with a feeding tube through his nose, connected to so many machines and IV running into his foot.

It was hard to see him in that situation again, but in my heart there was a feeling of immense gratitude again, and I didn't even think about what had happened the day before. He had survived one more challenge. He was receiving the best care possible. I had saved his life. It was Christmas evening. Not the way I had planned, nor where I had planned but I couldn't have asked for a better experience to feel love and support on that night.

For many years growing up, Stel and his family donated toys to Sick Kids hospital. As a teenager, he started going with his friends to the cancer floor to hand out the toys himself. Before we had kids, I knew that story. We even went together one year.

In 2012, we became recipients of the toys that were donated to the hospital. A nurse came into our room and asked me how many children we had. I said two. She gave me two vouchers and directed me to the toy room. When I got there, I cried. It was the most beautiful room filled with toys, books, stuffed animals and video games. There was even a wrapping table. I could choose toys for my both kids and wrap them. They knew that when parents have a sick child, the last thing they have time to do is to go out to buy toys. They made sure not only Gabriel would get a toy, but Thomas would as well.

I went back to the PICU and I showed Stel the two bags of toys; we cried together in gratitude. We felt such love for the complete strangers who made sure their donations would make a difference in someone's life. This time they had made a difference in our lives. Without a word, we hugged and we knew we had to give back somehow one day.

On Christmas day, Santa and his elves came to visit Gabriel in the room and brought a teddy bear. We took pictures with them and the bear. Gabriel was too sick to even see Santa. We celebrated that moment. We celebrated our first Christmas as a family of four, even if it was a bit disjointed. Thomas had stayed with Stel's family and we took turns, spending a couple of hours with him, then returning to Gabriel.

I also made time to go to the NICU at Mount Sinai to hug whoever was working that day. I was in a state of total gratitude for them one more time. Through the Family Integrated Care program, which is now the culture at Mount Sinai, I had become empowered. That program had given me the knowledge and skills to do what I did to save his life.

The PICU at Sick Kids is a very intense place. However, my husband, who always made me laugh, kept me laughing even in acute circumstances. While all the parents in the PICU were very stressed out, and we were too, Stel managed to crack his jokes. He still shared his positive energy, joking with the nurses and the ladies at the front desk. He has an incredible ability to lighten up any room and make people feel inspired.

Gabriel was discharged on the night of December 31st, just in time for a fresh start in a new year. I had a good feeling about the coming year.

As I was growing up, my mom repeatedly told me stories about the hardships she had in her life. She told these stories, but never from a place of victimhood or feeling sorry for herself. She always saw a different perspective than most. She saw the difference between what could be changed and what could not. She accepted, with serenity, the things she could not change. What she always did was change the way she responded to what happened. She would always choose a more positive outlook to cope with the things she didn't have any control over.

I had never given any thought about how my mom dealt with the adversities of her life. After the NICU and PICU, our long conversations of the past came to surface and I analyzed how my mom had been dealing with the events of her own life. It was a moment of profound learning for me to realize that she always accepted what was, with the idea in mind that she had the power to take a different path if she chose to. This was vital for me to comprehend in this new chapter of my life because I would be confronted with many new *normals*. The faster I surrendered and accepted what I couldn't change, the easier it would be.

CHAPTER 12
Rebirth

"Great things are done by a series of small things brought together."
— *Vincent Van Gogh*

Stel worked all day and Thomas was in school full time. I didn't speak with other people very much during those days. My daily contact was with Voula and Kerri, my NICU buddies who had also been recently discharged from Mount Sinai. We had created a very strong bond. We all coped with the NICU differently, but always encouraged one another to keep going.

January and February were very cold months with a lot of snow. I watched from my window, as the snowflakes fell. I always loved to watch it from inside, feeling the warmth of my house. Other than doctor appointments and follow up clinics, I was mostly at home. I could look back and reflect on the NICU days. I took the time to re-evaluate my life. I looked at my present life, my new normal, and all the events that led me to where I was. I looked at how much I had grown and learned. I looked at my husband and my children. I needed that time to process all that happened.

I had to deal with negative emotions of sadness and fear that kept showing up. I also had to grieve for my son Michael. I knew that when I felt fear, I was thinking about the future, about what could happen to Gabriel. I had to develop mental muscle to be constantly present in my daily life. It takes time to become proficient at that process, as we are not taught to think that way. I made a decision that what happened wouldn't define who I was. I had decided not to live in fear or have sadness inside me. As I stated before, I believe that nothing is inherently good or bad; it is what we make of it, how we respond to what happens.

A conversation I had with one of Gabriel's doctors triggered my decision to act in the present moment and not wait for the wounds to heal in time. It was the beginning of another spring when I had the appointment. Every follow up or new appointment was always about the baby and this one didn't start any different. He said that Gabriel was getting stronger and the pulmonary clinic at Sick Kids had started to wean him off of the oxygen. Dr. Jason, our naturopath doctor, looked deep in my eyes after he was done with Gabriel and asked me, "How are you doing?" I hadn't asked myself that in quite a long time. I didn't answer him because I really didn't know. He said to me, "Your son is now breathing better and it is time for you to get out of the fight or flight mode and start breathing again."

I went home and for many weeks I thought about his words. Doctor's words have an incredible power. The words spoken that day by Dr. Jason were no different. Each day, in our family room with Gabriel, where I would breastfeed him, play with him on the floor or just enjoy the miracle of life in him, I would think about Dr. Jason's words. In those moments, I was always present and so grateful to the life I had, reveling in each second.

My choice was to live fully for me, for my husband and for my beautiful children. I looked back on the memories of the NICU and I started my healing process there. I went over the ups and downs, evaluating the events, and realized that there were more great memories than other ones.

I was living in gratitude for my nurses Edna and Karen, for all the nurses I got to know there, for the doctors, for the cleaners, for the front desk ladies, for the RTs, for the social workers and for every single person involved in Gabriel's care and in the care of my family. It was that feeling that pushed me forward and to look at the NICU as the best experience I could have had in my life. Years later, I came to the realization that how well we experience the NICU is how well we will do afterward.

This evaluation process was profound for me. I knew Gabriel had come into my life for a reason. In the beginning, during the surviving days, I questioned why all of these things were happening to me. Those questions led me to the countless hours I spent talking to one of my mentors, Danny, who is in some sense, my spiritual coach. He reminded me over and over again that all of it is part of a contract that our soul agreed on before coming to this life. He constantly asked me if I could see myself signing this contract with Stel to accept Gabriel in our lives, facing all the challenges presented to us. My answer was and has always been yes, absolutely, and I would not change a thing. It's from a place of unconditional love that I can embrace what is.

Danny loves to talk and guide people to discover their spiritual paths. He believes and says that we are all divine and come from the light. However, we tend to forget this. Further, he taught me that as part of our own evolution we are given challenges to see how we manage. If we succeed, we can then take one step further, in our spiritual journey.

Many times in our conversations, I laugh, saying that I've had enough challenges, and with a very calm voice while holding my hand he says, "Sweetheart, you are doing just fine." He always reminds me to quiet my monkey mind and free myself from my worries. I feel stronger when I talk to him, as if my soul remembers the contract I had signed before this life.

On Gabriel's first birthday, May 17th, 2013, we went to the NICU to celebrate his first year with those who helped him through his first few months. The nurses love to see how the babies develop after they leave the NICU. It was a great visit! We had a lot to celebrate. Being alive was already a reason to celebrate, but even more, we were a family that was fully alive and thriving. That day, Stel and I remembered the decision that we made the previous Christmas to give back to the hospitals that supported us. We declared that our first initiative would be to do something for the families at Christmas. The idea still needed to be fully planned, but it was the beginning of a long-term commitment in support of Mount Sinai and Sick Kids, the hospitals that saved our Gabriel.

We marked his first birthday with a big party inspired by the book *Oh, the Places You'll Go!* by Dr. Seuss. I had read this book hundreds of times to Gabriel in the NICU. It's a great story about the journey of life and its challenges. I was still cautious about Gabriel's health and tried to limit his contact with other kids up to that point. I made sure everyone who was invited to the party was healthy. I had hand sanitizer at the front door, welcoming 45 children. It was the first time our friends' kids and cousins met Gabriel. It was a celebration of life, of his life, of our lives. We had all made it through the first year. It was the re-birth of our family. One week later, I couldn't have received better news to embrace the re-birth. Cathy, the nurse-practitioner from the Pulmonary Clinic at Sick Kids Hospital, sent an e-mail that made us all proud and ready to start a new chapter. Here was her short message:

"Good afternoon Fabiana...the oximetry report looks great...go ahead and take away the oxygen :)"

We were all sitting in the living room. Stel was holding Gabriel. My parents were visiting and Thomas was playing at our feet. When I read the e-mail, we all jumped up in excitement. We opened a bottle of champagne and had a candlelight dinner that evening. Due to Gabriel being on oxygen, we couldn't have open flames in the house while the tanks were working.

That was the day I really started to breathe again. This time breathing with confidence that it was time to move forward and pursue all the dreams and goals I had once set. This time I had a different perspective. I was looking at the future with my eyes and my heart fully present, completely in the now. That was the main difference in the way I had decided to move forward. It was a new beginning for me and for my family.

Stel and I spent time adjusting to each other and reconnecting as a couple. Our schedules had taken us apart for so long. When Gabriel was in hospital, I spent the days with him. Stel waited until I came home, before leaving to go to the hospital himself, during the week. I joked that he did the night shift. He got to know all the night nurses. He became friends with Voula's husband, Bill, and they had a Greek party every night. They both brought food and drinks for the nurses. This is what Greeks do to thank people who help them. We spent very little time together, with the exception of Sundays, when Stel brought Thomas to see Gabriel. Some days I was angry with him because I was missing him. I was missing us being a couple, but didn't have the energy to deal with it at that point.

After the discharge, I moved to Gabriel's bedroom because of the oxygen. I bought a daybed so I could watch the monitor all night. We didn't have time to talk about us, our feelings, about the way we had been dealing with the stress of the situation. It put a lot of stress on our marriage. I was in a mama bear mode for so long, thinking that I was the only one able to care for Gabriel that I had pushed Stel aside. We both felt disconnected from one another. Our decision to move forward made us talk and reconnect. It was hard work for both of us.

My loving husband planned a three-day trip to London, England, to celebrate our 10th anniversary, it was magical as our story really started there. On that trip, we connected heart-to-heart again and spoke candidly about what had happened; how he coped with the NICU. With an open heart, he told me that he didn't know his place in all that had happened. I told him that I was angry with him many days because he wasn't there during the day and he reminded me that this is what men do. They go into the cave and his cave was to work hard to make sure our family was supported financially. We understood that we both had to heal from the experience. The NICU tested our marriage but we were committed to stay together and work through it, we started to dedicate more time for each other, becoming stronger as a consequence.

I continued to set even more new goals. I had so many dreams of helping people in so many ways when I was growing up. I always dreamed that one day, when I had enough qualifications, time or more money, I would help. There was never a good time to start the things I wanted to do, I was always focused on something else. This time was different. Understanding that *now* is all we have, I decided to start doing the things I wanted to do, immediately. They were big goals, which could be overwhelming, but this time I didn't over-think or spend days wondering how I would do it all. One of my inspirations was by Dr. Edson, my fertility doctor in Brazil. I asked one of his nurses if I could give away the remaining medication from my treatments. She said absolutely as he donates his time and the treatment to 100 couples a year who couldn't afford to pay.

I started to become more involved at Mount Sinai. Back at the hospital in a different role gave me a broader view on how every-thing works. It made me deepen my relationship with the medi-cal team, realizing how much they care about their patients and families. I got to know the visionaries who work non-stop to im-prove health care and the outcomes for the families. I started to work with the doctors who had saved Gabriel's life. I became part of different programs and different initiatives and I became the ambassador of Family Integrated Care because it shaped who I've become.

Setting new goals and purposefully giving back provided me with more energy to be able to carry on in my journey with Gabriel. We were still fully booked with appointments and follow-ups with doctors as well as therapists, but I made time to help those in need. The more I helped, the more energy I had to give my family.

Around the time when I was setting my new goals, we noticed that Gabriel's motor development was delayed and I was attempting to *fix* him. I really wanted him to catch up. I was searching for ther-apies, traditional and also what is considered alternative. I tried many different options. I wanted to maximize his potential. He was so young and I believed in his ability to reach all the mile-stones for babies.

I was focused on his therapies and my activities at Mount Sinai while trying to balance some fun time with Thomas and keep my marriage alive. It was physically exhausting at times, going from place to place, organizing activities, going on late date nights with very few hours of sleep, but my purpose to give back was driving me full force. I had to continue.

CHAPTER 13
Thriving

"We are but visitors on this planet. We are here for ninety or one hundred years at the very most. During that period, we must try to do something good, something useful with our lives. If you contribute to other people's happiness, you will find the true goal, the true meaning of life."

– H.H. The 14th Dalai Lama

Recently, my friend and mentor, Teresa, sent me a beautiful story to read that illustrates what I believe to be true on how problems and challenges can change and transform us for the better.

"Don't worry if you have problems; which is easy to say until you are in the midst of a big one, I know. But the only people I am aware of who don't have troubles are gathered in little neighborhoods. Most communities have at least one. We call them cemeteries.

If you are breathing you have difficulties. It is the way of life. And believe it or not, most of your problems may actually be good for you. Let me explain. Maybe you have seen the Great Barrier Reef, stretching some 1,800 miles from New Guinea to Australia. Tour guides regularly take visitors to view the reef. On one tour, the guide was asked an interesting question: "I noticed that the lagoon side of the reef looks pale and lifeless, while the ocean side is vibrant and colorful", a traveler observed. "Why is this?" The guide gave an interesting answer: "The coral around the lagoon side is in still water, with no challenge for its survival. It dies early. The coral on the ocean side is constantly being tested by wind, waves and storms – surges of power. It has to fight for survival every day of its life. As it is challenged and tested, it changes and adapts. It grows healthy. It grows strong. And it reproduces." Then he added this telling note: "That is the way it is with every living organism." That is how it is with people. Challenged and tested, we come alive. Like coral pounded by the sea, we grow. Physical demands can cause us to grow stronger. Mental and emotional stress can produce tough-mindedness and resiliency. Spiritual testing can produce strength of character and faithfulness. So, you have problems. Just tell yourself, "There I grow again."

I knew I had grown a lot since my experience in the NICU and I was about to be tested again by the storm. Certainly, I still had more room to grow.

Three months before Gabriel turned two years old, I went to a follow-up clinic at Mount Sinai. It was his 18 month, corrected age, follow-up. I loved going to appointments there, as every time I was able to show him off in the NICU. That day was different; I had no idea that on February 27, 2014, Gabriel would receive the diagnosis of cerebral palsy. Despite of all of the learning I had done in the past, I did not know how to respond to this unexpected, life-changing news. I let my body react. One more time, I couldn't breathe. I wanted to run out of the hospital as fast as I could. I was alone with Gabriel. I didn't even think about asking Stel to come with me. I usually take him to appointments by myself unless it's an important appointment. I didn't consider a follow-up to be *that* important.

I had been working with Dr. Jennifer on a project at Sinai for two months and she was the in-service doctor that day. She spoke to me with a lot of caution and compassion, gently asked me if I had heard of cerebral palsy. Of course, I had, but I didn't think my son would have it. I thought I could fix whatever was going on with him, but those words, that label, made me feel that my trials had all been in vain. It sounded so definitive.

Once again, I drove home down College Street, the same street I had driven hundreds of times before. I had flashbacks of the days I was driving to and from the NICU. I felt a tightness in my heart. I was picking up Maiara – an amazing young woman who had been helping me with Gabriel – on my way home. She came into our lives during a time of transition, adapting to our house and developing a very strong bond with Gabriel. As soon as she got into the car I burst into tears. I told her about the diagnosis and she asked me what it meant. I didn't know what to say. I didn't know what it meant, either. We were both at a loss for words. I called Stel to tell him and I don't even remember what either of us said.

Between tears, Maiara and I sat down on the floor of my family room with Gabriel laying down between us. We searched the Internet, to see what we could learn about cerebral palsy. I started to watch videos on YouTube. They made me feel, at the same time, great despair and hope.

Cerebral Palsy, in very simple terms, is the lack of muscle control due to an injury of the developing brain. There is no cure. Doctor Jennifer said that when I read her report, it would sound worse than it actually is. I got her report a few weeks later, the official diagnosis was Spastic Quadriplegia Cerebral Palsy. At that point I didn't care to know about the spastic quadriplegia part. I focused on the cerebral palsy part and I was devastated.

Stel came home and we talked about it. He said it was just a label. It took me a few weeks to wrap my head around it. Tema, Gabriel's osteopath, who became a good friend, reassured me that it was just a label as well. After all, he was the same boy he was the day before the diagnosis. It still took some time to digest this news, and while I did, I kept repeating Danny's words in my head: *It's all part of the contract.* I knew it was to help me grow and change. It made me calm and gave me comfort.

The lessons from the NICU came back to me. They really transformed my reality, as I stated before. I accepted my new normal faster this time around. Letting go of the fear of the future for Gabriel and for us as a family, put me at ease almost immediately. I was constantly monitoring my thoughts and making sure I was living in the now, focusing on the good things happening around us. In the NICU I learned to live in a state of gratitude and it became my new way of living and until now, every day before I go to bed I write down three things that I'm grateful for in that day, even if it is a very small thing. It immediately changes the focus for the better.

Once again, I reminded myself that everything is neutral; the situation is neutral, like a blank canvas. I'm the one who gives the meaning and chooses the colors and shape. The problem is not really a problem; it is the story we choose to create around the neutral situation that could be the problem.

Once again, it would be the beginning of another new normal. What that label really meant in everyday life, we were yet to discover. The first steps were to embrace it, stay present, continue to celebrate Gabriel, and look at the possibilities.

It was a learning process for me to understand what the disability meant. I had to learn about cerebral palsy, CP, and how it affected Gabriel's motor development. After one year, I decided to focus on what *Spastic* and *Quadriplegia* meant. I knew all along that quadriplegia meant four, but when I translated it into Portuguese, *Tetraplegico*, I realized that unlike what doctor Jennifer had said, he had been highly affected. It meant that Gabriel's CP had compromised all four of limbs, the arms and legs. I actually laughed that it took so long for that to hit me.

Despite Gabriel's brain damage, I worked hard to remember the gift of life. I kept in mind how far he had come and kept my faith in how far I believed he could go. He beat the odds so many times in his short life, I know he will continue to do so. I do everything I can to support him and to provide him with a better quality of life. I no longer try to fix him as I have realized he is not broken. I don't see my child as disabled. I see him with different abilities and I choose to focus on what he can do. I fully accept who he is and celebrate his life, every day.

It is not always easy, the endless appointments, overwhelming medical explanations, trying to understand and navigate the system, do my own research on new treatments and therapies and lack of sleep affect me physically and mentally. The only effective way that I have found to deal with the daily challenges, is to address them when they come. As a family, we work together to find solutions. Being flexible and adapting as things occur has helped all of us to find our roles in the new normals we must live.

Thomas also had to adapt to his new role as a big brother. He had the expectation that Gabriel would be running and playing games with him. He too had to deal with his anger and frustration until he fully accepted his brother. In his own way, he keeps finding solutions to play with Gabriel. The bond between them is indescribable. And I know, he will always advocate for and celebrate his brother. Being a sibling of a child with special needs is not an easy task. Many times, he gets left aside because Gabriel's needs are so high. He often needs to answer his friends' questions about why his brother doesn't walk. However, he carries the pride of being a big brother and he likes to show off his brother in school and at other activities we attend. I know all that he is learning and seeing is making him a better human being.

Stel and I decided that we would still do everything we had planned before having kids, such as travelling, biking, attending sports events, and so far we have managed to do so. We need to be more creative and plan ahead of time and our question is always how we can do it.

Throughout the challenges, I became aware of my thoughts and emotions. Although there is resistance to go back to my old pattern of becoming sad and feeling fear, I consciously put myself in a positive state by focusing on all the things I consider to be good in my life right now, remembering that everything is love and knowing everything is possible.

Today, I share my journey, which is not over, my struggles and my victories openly. Once again, it helps me to normalize my situation just as much it did when I was going through the fertility treatment. I know that when I share my reality and make myself vulnerable, I encourage others to speak up, to share their story. I believe it is a good way to start the healing process and acceptance of what is, instead of bottling up the negative emotions.

Life becomes turbulent at times and it can be hard and traumatic but when we look for the joy in the journey, the biggest struggle can become the biggest gift. No matter what happens, everyone will laugh and love again, life carries on and everything will fall into place and a new story will be created.

As I rewrite my own story, I see that everything has come full circle for me. My desire to change the world growing up seemed such a big task, but I have realized that changing the world is helping or supporting one person at a time which creates a ripple effect making the world around us a better place. And we all have the power to positively impact someone's life. My goal is to inspire change and impact the lives of families who are going through adversities by showing them the possibilities at the time they are blindsided. I learned that we are all stronger than we think and when I talk to others I show them that it is possible to get back on their feet after having all their hopes and dreams destroyed. My involvement with the hospital and other charity initiatives makes me feel alive, it gives meaning to my life and fulfills my purpose.

I see life beyond myself; it gives me a bigger picture instead of worrying about small things and what people think of me. Through this transformation, I have experienced freedom and I learned to live authentically.

Just like the caterpillar inside the cocoon where it is dark and tight, the caterpillar must surrender to the process, and with time it breaks free; it grows transforming into a butterfly.

One of my favorite quotes is by Trina Paulus and depicts the journey I have lived. When asked how one would go about becoming a butterfly, this is the answer given: "You must want to fly so much that you are willing to give up being a caterpillar."

The adversities I faced made me break free from old paradigms and patterns of thinking and behavior. They transformed me and supported me in rediscovering who I really am. They gave my existence higher purpose. As I thrive, my family thrives. No matter what challenges and adversities one faces, anyone can go from surviving to thriving, the choice however, is yours.

ACKNOWLEDGMENTS

In my career as a journalist, my job was to find stories. I did not think that one day I would be telling my own. I hope my story can inspire others to rise above their challenges to live a more purposeful life.

I also did not think that I would need to learn medical terminology to survive, but circumstances led me there and I feel empowered to advocate for my son because of the knowledge I have gained.

There are many people I'm grateful for in my life. First and foremost, to my parents. They gave me a strong foundation and taught me compassion.

To my husband Stel - thank you for being my rock. Thank you for your patience, unconditional love and support. Thank you for making me laugh even in the most stressful of situations. Thank you for pushing me out of my comfort zone and believing in me. I couldn't have chosen a better person to share this bumpy road with.

To the amazing NICU team at Mount Sinai Hospital - I have no words to express my gratitude to each and every one of you. My life has changed more than I could ever imagine – for the better. Thank you for guiding me on every step of the way and welcoming me as part of your team. Thank you Dr. Shoo Lee for being such a visionary and for leading the best NICU team in the world. Your groundbreaking pilot study *Family Integrated Care* was the key element for me to survive 146 days in the NICU. Thank you Dr. Jennifer Young, Dr. Sharon Unger, Dr. Karel O'Brien, Marianne Bracht and Kristy MacDonell for trusting me and letting me be part of your research and projects. It means a lot to me. Marianne, thank you for your dedication to what you do and for teaching me the skill that allowed me to save Gabriel's life. You are an extraordinary human being. Lastly, my primary nurses who never left my side, Karen Walsh and Edna Azanza (you will always be alive in my heart). Thank you both for teaching me how to be a mom in the hospital. I will always love you.

To Dr. David Chitayat - thank you for your love and guidance when I was most vulnerable and scared during my pregnancy.

To the Sick Kids Hospital team - especially Lora Carinci, Dr. Steven Miller, Cathy Daniels, Arlene Chaves, Dr. Theo Moraes, Dr. Nasrin Tehrani and the emergency team, thank you. Your commitment to improve the life of my child will always be appreciated. I'm grateful to have the best team caring for Gabriel.

To my dear friends that I have known the longest - thank you for keeping me in your lives even though my time dedicated to you is so limited. Thank you for your beautiful messages and on-going support. Chantalone Smith, Renata Runge and Emma Eriksson – your help, in particular on the most critical times, will never be forgotten.

To my new friends and the special needs moms and dads, especially from the Three-To-Be Foundation - thank you for your encouragement, for sharing your resources and for keeping our community active when advocating for our children.

To the amazing women who inspire me to do more for others - Claire Kerr-Zlobin, Kate Robson, Dana Kim, Debbie Sutherland and Shelley Neal, thank you for easing the way for others.

To my mentors: Teresa Easler and Joan Emery - thank you for holding me accountable, sharing your wisdom and for giving me your time so generously. And to Gina Mollicone-Long - thank you for helping me discover my greatness.

To all the therapists, respite workers and volunteers who take care of Gabriel - thank you for believing and for creating possibilities for him. Especially, Tema Stein - thank you for showing me the options in my new world. You are one of a kind.

To the team at Silver Creek Preschool – thank you for loving my child and seeing his potential.

To Maiara Morosini and Paula da Paz – if it takes a village to raise a child, you are it. Thank you for being my village and for loving my kids as your own.

To my son Thomas – thank you for challenging me to be a better mom. I hope that one day, all the things that you have experienced since an early age will teach you how to be a compassionate human being. I watch in awe, how you interact with other kids who have different abilities. I love seeing the bond between you and Gabriel, and how much you love him and protect him. I'm very proud of you.

To my son Gabriel – thank you choosing me as your mom and providing me the opportunity to grow. You have taught me the most invaluable life lessons, including how to make those lessons come alive, daily.